A MAG FOR ALL SEASONS

Billy Furious

Mag Publishing

'To all the people who make going to the match a brilliant experience, even when Newcastle lose.'

Contents

CHAPTER 1

Welcome To Newcastle

This is a true story from the city of Newcastle upon Tyne.

Let's not beat around the bush here - Newcastle is a fuckin' brilliant city. It vibrates with energy, it positively crackles with life and unless you're some pig ignorant snob or an inbred, knuckle-dragging half-witted twat it's impossible not to fall hopelessly in love with the place. Most are born to this love and never question it because it's part of their being. They know they are lucky to have such a home, are fiercely proud and protective of the place and thrive on its many magnificent gifts.
Others discover it and never want to leave. People come to study, visit or work and stay for ten years or forever. Those who leave in search of work or for love or for whatever reason, return with a lump in the throat to the airport, with hammering heart over the river on the train or with a tear in the eye by car over the Tyne Bridge. The Tyne Bridge at night glows like a magical gateway, the lights from the quayside and other bridges flicker about you as you cross and the city stands proud before you with open arms and heart, welcoming you to your one true home.

The pulsating energy of the city, its lifeblood, is its people. The people are passionate - even the miserable, cynical, grumpy or violent people are miserable, cynical, grumpy or violent with passion. Most are prepared to work hard, play hard, laugh at hardship and take the piss out of anything that moves, especially themselves. There is no obvious hierarchy and if you think there is you will end up embarrassed or on your arse - the phrase, "Do you know who I am?" will get an "I don't give a fuck......" answer in Newcastle faster than anywhere else in the Western world. And that's got to be a good thing.
Of course it's got its rough areas, where hasn't? I'm not trying to paint a picture of a daisy-filled, sun-drenched dream land where the happy faces

8

children eat kitten shaped lollipops all the livelong day (the weather's generally too shite for that). You can get as much trouble as you want if you know where to look but if you don't want any, chances are you won't get any. The locals are friendly but you will be expected to give and receive abuse with confidence and a smile.

Like everywhere, Newcastle has got places it's best to stay away from - places where you take your life in your hands simply by walking through - the city centre on a Saturday for example, where ugly, stupid, hateful people will deliberately stand in shop doorways with their screaming children allowing no citizen to enter or leave without running the gauntlet of passive smoke, pushchairs and walking sticks.

There are places in the UK where pubs don't bother opening on a Sunday night because people don't go out. In Newcastle the weekend lasts from Thursday evening until last thing Sunday night and drinks are cheap most places on Monday for the students if you can still hack the pace. When somebody finally does something about the dumb fucking licensing laws Newcastle will finally be free to be the 24 hour party city it aches to be. The place will be off-the-leash crazy and will rock like Val Doonican in an earthquake (ask your grandad).

The heartbeat that pumps the blood is Newcastle United Football Club. The fortunes of the football team dictates the mood of the city from unbearable despondency to utter euphoria, the emotion emanating from St James's Park sweeps all before it. From the very young to the infirm and ancient, people know the players, the form, the most recent score and how that affects the club's season. Football in Newcastle is not seen as a hobby, or a pastime or an interest - it's recognised as a 24 hour life consuming obsession. There may still be places in this country where it is possible for godless people to ignore the national game in these Skytastic, constant info-bombardment days but you never could in Newcastle.

Now after years of media saturation it seems hard to imagine a time when being seen to be a football supporter meant you must be some kind of lunatic, drunken sadist to be avoided at all cost. It was never like that in Newcastle, it was and is always assumed that if you come from Newcastle you are a Newcastle fan.

And if you're not? You damn well better have a damn good reason for it.

Consequently, getting back to a city centre bar after an away game you were always made to feel special. Like you were some returning hero who had been off representing everybody else and you would be quizzed for details and your word would be the first hand truth. Even now when the game has been seen by all either on Sky or in a packed pub showing Norwegian or Dutch TV, the fans at the match feel as though they are entitled to the last word, this despite the fact that they have actually had the worst available view.

The fans at the game get to witness so much more than what the television camera deems to show and we all know that our judgement of that dodgy offside decision is the right one. Even if the incident in question took place at the opposite end of the ground whilst we were in the bog.

It's in that strange far-off time that this story begins. Before Sky Television. Before marketing managers. Before all-seater stadia and designer club leisurewear. Before the Premier League and repackaged family orientated days out. Before you could get in The Champions League by finishing fourth and before end of season highlights on interactive DVD.

A mythical half-forgotten time when we really and truly feared that the city's heart would stop beating. Forever.

CHAPTER 2

Shit Or Bust

Newcastle United had been in decline for a while. In 1989 the club got relegated from the top flight. Jim Smith rebuilt the team and packed it full of experienced players designed to get the club up again. Smith provided us with the best footballing side in the Division and we battered the crap out of Leeds and Sheffield United, the two clubs who won automatic promotion. Failing on the last day of the regular season we were condemned to the play-offs where we suffered a painful and cruel loss to sunderland in the semi-final. The following season "experienced" quickly became "old", Smith's gamble had failed, our momentum and exuberance ground to a painful rusty halt and he left. Ossie Ardiles came as manager and within months had fielded the youngest ever first team in Newcastle United's history. Then he managed to put out a younger one early in the following season.

Damn, we were fiercely proud of that team, made up as it was of so many young local lads, who played with a swagger and a passion the fans could identify with. Ardiles had no luck with injuries that season but the truth was that team couldn't defend to save its bastard life. We were at entirely the wrong end of the division and while we refused to believe that the club could be relegated into the Third Division it was in fact a dangerous and very real prospect.

In what appeared to be an act of utter desperation, Chairman John Hall sacked the still popular Ardiles and brought in former player and former England captain Kevin Keegan.

Keegan's arrival as an untried manager at such a desperate time caused a great deal of argument but the people responded passionately and the team exploded away from danger. An unattended virgin during a Viking invasion will not get carried away quicker than Newcastle fans after a couple of victories, especially with Keegan stoking the flames, and odds were quoted for promotion. We were going to rampage through the Division until (and not for the last time) the wheels came spinning off. The initial adrenalin faded, the bad luck and appalling defending came back and dropped us right down into the shite again. Keegan walked out in a temper because the few brass buttons promised and required to bring Brian Kilcline in to bolster the defence had disappeared. John Hall's wife, Lady May, reportedly pulled £200,000 out of her handbag, Keegan came back, "Killer" Kilcline signed and immediately improved the defence but the performances overall became fitful and desperate.

With just two games left we were still right in it. Our last home game against Portsmouth was 0-0 with seconds remaining, the crowd split between utter hysteria and morose resignation, when David Kelly blasted one of the most important goals in NUFC history into the Portsmouth net. The crowd went utterly ballistic with relief and joy but later quiet consideration of the League table revealed that we probably still needed a result at promotion-chasing Leicester to ensure our survival.

A day of surreal weirdness began with usually hostile Middlesbrough fans giving us thumbs up signs and waving on the A1. The top of the table was as tight as the bottom and us tripping up Leicester would do Boro a big favour. Yet still open signs of friendship from Boro supporters were (and are) as rare as tap dancing dodos on your wardrobe - and it was equally unnerving to witness.

Leicester is the type of scabby one-eyed bastard hole of a place that most of us wouldn't dream of visiting if not for the love of our football team. The place is a gutter on Shit Street and packs of home fans wander like mongrel dogs after the apocalypse looking for someone weaker or smaller in numbers to prey on.

Undeterred, as ever, we found a pub but you wouldn't drown a diseased goat in the beer, it was so foul and the locals were getting fidgety so we went to the ground where our players were warming up and some locals were running laps of the pitch for charity. We happily abused the ones with the most notable features, "You Fat Bastard", and, "There's Only One Jimmy Saville", being the extent of our wit - we jeered Frank Worthington and cheered Kevin Keegan and Terry McDermott when they joined in.

Our support numbered only 1,800. The demand for tickets had been astronomical and much gnashing of teeth had occurred over the way the tickets were allocated. Today the club does a pretty good job of getting tickets to the most deserving fans with a computer-based system that reportedly tracks the amount of games you've been to. The majority of travelling fans didn't have season tickets then because they preferred to stand at home games and only a very small section of St James's had standing season ticket holders. NUFC's official travel club also got an allocation so providing you were early enough to the ground you could join that and get a ticket having never been to an away game before in your life.

Ticket distribution is one improvement in our lives, as is not having to go to Filbert Street any more is undeniably another. The narrow strip of tickets the away fans got which stretched along one half of the side of the pitch was barely fit for cattle, never mind cattle who wanted to see a game of football. Things were made even worse by the fact that the busy little bees of Leicester City had spent the week going up to the game building a six foot fence in front of our enclosure.

We were twisted with nerves but in strong confident voice. We cheered the names as our team was read out but shook our heads at each other because Keegan seemed to have opted for skill above brawn and this was going to be a war.

The notable exception led our team out. Brian "Killer" Kilcline. 8 feet tall, long straggly hair hanging way past shoulders as broad as a fat girl's wardrobe. Beard wild and unkempt he had a look in his eye and a purpose in his stride that gave us all heart. His whole appearance screamed, "You might score Leicester, but you're going to have to get past me to do it and that is NOT going to fucking well happen."

The Leicester fans in end of season party mood with three points guaranteed against a team from the bottom of the Division released their blue and white balloons, happily tossed their ticker-tape onto the pitch and their loose change at the away fans.

Our supporters at the front quickly climbed the new fence to get a decent view, which left the rest of us standing on the backs of our plastic seats trying to get a glimpse of anything.

I wobbled and looked behind me. "That's a nun." Newcastle fans often dress as nuns at the end of the season - because they also wear black and white or because some of our fans are perverse sexual deviants but this was a little old lady - a proper nun smiling benignly despite the fact that she wouldn't have been able to see a square foot of grass never mind a footballer.

We sang, we shouted, we wobbled precariously. A Leicester defender underhit a backpass and Gavin Peacock, our man of the season, was onto it. He clipped the ball into the net with supreme confidence then wheeled away towards us.

I have a framed picture of him running away after scoring that goal that still gladdens my heart ten years later. One arm aloft, easy smile, on the angle of his run. At the time? Bedlam! Total fuckin' chaos. We screamed and yelled for joy as the plastic of the seats twisted, buckled, snapped and shattered beneath our flailing feet. Blows were exchanged with some Leicester fans who sneaked behind some stewards to get at the Mags to our right.

Coins whizzed at us and I was hit on the side of the head with a warm sticky brown substance that I was relieved to discover was mince and onion.

"STAYING UP, STAYING UP, STAYING UP," we sang for ourselves . "STAYING DOWN, STAYING DOWN, STAYING DOWN," we shouted at the Leicester fans - one of whom, a very fat man, became apoplectic with rage and gesticulated wildly with his fingers. One of our lads picked up a discarded balloon, stuffed it up his jumper , puffed out his cheeks and paraded up and down by the fence that separated us until the fat fucker was scarlet with rage as even his own fans laughed. With our emotions already running high it seemed like the funniest thing ever.

On the pitch Leicester got shambolic and nervous but our second goal wouldn't come. Conflicting scores were coming in from other games and confusion and nervousness grew. But nothing else mattered - if we won we were safe. Time had crawled out of our comprehension - the sun dazzled our eyes but we were still OK. Then a long ball was lifted towards our goal - there could only be a few minutes left. We failed to clear it. Oh God, we've seen this too often. The ball bounced back and forth across the face of our goal until it was bundled into our net.

Leicester fans swarmed across the pitch in their hundreds. Many came towards us - some Newcastle fans tried to climb over the fence to get at them. Mental. The police came out in force to help the stewards clear the pitch then formed a tight line in front of us which made our obscured view even worse. Leicester fans were on the grass by the touchline waiting to reinvade the pitch on the final whistle. "Oxford are winning," I heard, which was bad news.

The Newcastle fans redoubled their efforts. My voice cracked, the sun and the sweat were stinging my eyes and I thought, "this is it, we're finished." John Hall had said the club could fold if we got relegated - perhaps it wouldn't have. Something could probably have been done but the damage would have been colossal. At the time it felt like we were helplessly watching the end of the world. Our goalkeeper Tommy Wright pumped the ball forward. It was over the top of everybody and a Leicester defender was making sure of its safe passage back to his keeper. He had reckoned without Gavin Peacock's belief in lost causes and Gav sprinted after this one like his life depended on it. The defender panicked and tried to help the ball back, the keeper was wrong-footed and the ball bobbled past him towards the empty net.

It's going in.

It's going wide.

One of their supporters, standing so very close to the post, is going to kick it away. It ran into the net and time that had slowed down to a crawl and sound that had vanished both exploded back. The roar from the 1,800 was insane with pleasure and relief. The hugs were random and the seating was splintered in the mayhem.

The Leicester fans were less pleased. Enraged, they swarmed towards us across the pitch in their thousands. The players stood in shock for a second then the Newcastle training staff urged them off the pitch. They fled towards Kevin Keegan and the tunnel. David Kelly, former Leicester player, however, was in trouble. His route to safety was cut off and his danger obvious. He ran the other way, a horde of angry blue and white jackals on his tail and vaulted into the safety of the Newcastle fans. Some of whom were clearly up for a counter-charge despite being outnumbered 200 to 1.

It's at the rare times like these that you appreciate the section of massive drunken fuckers who follow the Mags. It's all very well writing stiff letters to the papers afterwards but at the time you want as many great big hairy arsed, fearless buggers who look like they can punch holes in brick walls as possible. The police formed then reinforced a line between the two sets of fans. Given that we were all embracing each other and singing happily behind the fence it seemed bizarre that the newly arrived police video camera teams chose to point their equipment at us rather than at the murderous horde behind them, all of whom seemed intent on our physical harm. More important than that, was the game over, had we won? The week before at Stoke a similar incident there had been followed by the stadium being cleared and the match played to a conclusion - what the hell was going on?

And what happened to that nun?

CHAPTER THREE

Aftermath

Here in the 21st Century we take pretty much for granted the board that the fourth official holds up telling everybody how many minutes of injury time are to be played at the end of each half. The amount of time added by the referee still appears to be entirely arbitrary and you are still more likely to get a 6 flashing up on the board when you are clinging on to an undeserved point or three at Old Trafford or Highbury than anywhere else but at least you know. Back then we had no idea - I was convinced the game wasn't over and refused to leave. Wifey and some impatient policemen nudged me towards the exits while I scoured the players' tunnel for any signs of a sneaky ref peering out while all the players hid round a corner waiting for the ground to be declared empty so they could complete the allotted time.

I was possibly the last paying spectator to leave - by which time the referee, having decided to forgo the niceties of injury time, was probably hurrying towards his car pulling up his trousers and buttoning his shirt in a desperate attempt to get the fuck out of Dodge (well - Leicester) before anybody started asking awkward questions.

Outside was like the Wild West. The cavalry (Midlands constabulary) had circled the settlers wagons (supporters' buses) while the entire Apache Nation (unwashed spotty youths from Leicester) swarmed around us intent on murder.

Those outside the police cordon were left to fend for themselves while the wounded bled into handkerchiefs and the survivors bounced around hugging each other because the Toon were safe.

As it happened we could have lost and still stayed up - but that didn't matter - we had survived and now we needed to get home for beer.

The bus travellers were packed onto their coaches and the rest of us were marched off under heavy escort to the train station. Which was all well and good except Wifey and I had travelled in a car and our car mates were nowhere to be seen. It was half a mile before we managed to slip away from the police escort by which time we were hopelessly lost.

Two of us trying to look like we knew where we were going AND look miserable while packs of post-apocalyptic mongrel dogs in blue shirts eyed us suspiciously was hard enough, but.... look that's Trevor Brooking. Trevor Brooking, former gentleman of the West Ham and England midfield striding purposefully through the streets of Leicester, he would surely rush to our aid and give these scallywags a good clip round the ear if they set on us.

While the dogs were distracted by the former footballer we nipped off the other way, gathered our bearings and found that the one remaining car in the car park contained our unharmed comrades - engine running. We skulked out the city and raced up the motorway, scarves flapping out the window as we chattered up a ferocious thirst.

Later, everybody who went seemed to have a tale to tell. A friend, Les, had been talked into driving a transit to the game. His passengers had spent the journey south painting each others faces black and white, "it was like driving for a gang of badgers", he said, and they stuck out like a sore thumb trying to get away afterwards. Stuck at traffic lights the van was soon surrounded by Leicester fans banging on the windows like extras in a cheap zombie movie. The passenger door was opened by two lads, one of whom pulled a knife and said, "Come out to play Geordie". Les simply put his foot down and drove away - leaving the knife wielder spinning and his mate on the other side of the open door knocked clean into a plate glass window. Over the pavement and through a red light he didn't even look back.

Imagine our surprise when the papers went to war against the "Newcastle soccer louts" who had terrorised the poor people of sleepy Leicester. Random pictures of people in black and white shirts, helpfully provided by the Leicester police, "so-called fans" who had brought shame on the game. This despite the fact that somebody from Newcastle lost the sight in one eye from the barrage of missiles we had endured. I don't doubt for a second that some people threw stuff back but it was clearly us who had been under attack and now we were being stitched up.

Nobody cared.

Worse still Keegan had been very evasive about his future as our manager and had gone to ground. He'd done the job he came in to do but we were desperate for him to stay and other clubs were already circling over our few good players. Middlesbrough had been promoted to the shiny new Premier League and sunderland had managed to weasel their way into the Cup Final but still we felt our season had been a success and we wanted to build on it. All Kevin Keegan needed to do was tell us he loved us and that he was staying and we could enjoy life. A good start to this was Liverpool barely trying and still annihilating sunderland in the Cup Final. We had a party at our house to witness Michael Thomas and Ian Rush scoring the goals and we drank in their honour - watched the video of our recent victory over the mackems, went to the pub, played pool (very badly) and sang our heads off until we were asked politely by the manager to "shut the fuck up". Which we did.

For about a minute.

CHAPTER 4

Close Season

Some things don't change. The football season structures how you live your whole bloody life; where you need to be and when, what you can and can't do, everything. Non-footballing friends and family expect to not see you, or hear from you or at least get any sense out of you until the season's dust has well and truly settled. No matter how good or bad a season you have had, you are wrapped up in it until the last kick, utterly.

Then it's gone.

First thought: "Excellent, I can forget all about football, I can do the garden, fix the car, paint the front door, visit neglected relatives, take day trips to places of cultural interest."

Bollocks will you.

The same ongoing anxieties are there about the future of Newcastle United (short and long term) but without the essential cathartic release of meeting your mates and burning out your anxieties at the match.

You are abandoned in a sea of normal people doing normal things and you feel like you are just pretending to exist. You see other lost souls wearing a club shirt standing on Northumberland Street or in a garden centre gazing into the middle distance - completely cut off from reality.

You rush to buy papers for the slightest snippet of news, knowing full well they will provide little or no satisfaction - the club is empty, the players have all gone away and you are on your own. May as well dig the bastard garden.

In the summer of 92 the local papers did their best, painting a vivid and dramatic picture of an excitable band of NUFC directors pursuing Kevin Keegan across Europe, brandishing the contract that would keep him at the club. They were like the unshakeable posse that chase Butch Cassidy & The Sundance Kid across a continent's bare rock.

Keegan was run to ground in Spain and signed up, then reportedly the seemingly inexhaustible posse galloped south to France in pursuit of Chrissy Waddle. Waddler would surely be more than happy to give up Championships and European Cup finals at Marseille for a return to Newcastle. With Waddle in the team we would......... He signed for Sheffield Wednesday.

Every four years, hopeless football junkies can gorge themselves on a World Cup. Also at four yearly intervals we get the European Championships which, while lacking the exotic flavours of Japan v Jamaica or South Korea v USA, will just about keep us ticking over. A happy distraction. With real football.
In 1992 it was the European Championships. It's not the same rush as watching the Toon but it will keep you interested, especially if you have a bet. I personally put £5 of my last £10 in the world on Germany v Holland being a 2-2 draw. The other £5 I spent on strong lager. Holland scored their second goal, an equaliser in the last minute which meant I could afford to attend a good friend's wedding in Norfolk. The fact that I watched the game with Mark (Editor of popular Independent Newcastle Magazine 'The Mag' the finest, most fair minded and intelligent publication that is guaranteed to improve your mind and your sex life -subscribe now. Is that enough?) who had bet on Germany to win 2-1 made the event all the sweeter. Me jumping up and down on my sofa while he crawled around the floor blaming the German defence on an over consumption of sausages is a delightful and abiding memory.
On the down side, throwing your heart and soul into Graham Taylor's England was a frustrating and depressing waste of bloody time.
The success of Bobby Robson's 1990 World Cup campaign had ignited the national game with a new fervour and great things were expected of the legacy he left - but just two years later it fell desperately flat, England not even getting out of their group despite meticulous preparation. Denmark came in as a late replacement for the otherwise occupied Yugoslavia so all the Danish players had been drinking Carlsberg, eating cake and not even bothering to dig the garden like they had promised, until the day before the tournament began. They won the damn thing - what that tells us about meticulous preparation is a matter of opinion.
We watched the Final in The Barley Mow - regarded by many people at the time as the finest bar in the world. Unfortunately too far away from the football ground but permanently vibrant and busy with a veranda overlooking the Tyne. Hilariously surly and sarcastic barstaff would dispense cold drinks. In the summer - blissful. It was sold, done out (twice I think), the surly barstaff were replaced with the traditional disinterested students who never know who's next and somehow the magic, like all the customers, was lost. Refurbished &

renamed 'Stereo', it now has a dress code, ghastly live DJs, flashing lights and expensive drinks, just like half a million other pubs in the toon.

Whatever. On this evening the Final was on the telly and the bar was full but nobody seemed to be paying it much attention. Until Denmark scored and the place erupted. Seemed like everybody wanted the Danes to win (or more likely the Germans to lose) but didn't think they could. The Danes broke from seemingly relentless German pressure to score again and the place was jumping.

Again, no football for weeks, and then as now your "Idle-tittle-tattle-ometer" has to be switched on to maximum. Not just for tittle or, indeed, tattle but especially for outright lies and bullshit. Trouble is you can try and maintain a "believe nothing" attitude but your imagination runs away with you. Regular rumours of the imminent arrival of Rush, Hughes and Beardsley were more than we could bear.

The players we are teased with today are the likes of Rivaldo or Rui Costa which may tell you how football and Newcastle has changed but the mental struggle between believe nothing cynicism and pulse-racing wild imaginings is identical.

Now paying for your season ticket is like paying your car insurance or TV licence - it may seem a lot but there is no choice. Pay it or you're out and come the first game of the season somebody else will be in your seat. Up to 1992 you had a choice and many chose not to bother. Standing on the Gallowgate on a match to match basis was what we always did and we didn't have the cash or the inclination to change.

Then the local radio said Peter Beardsley was due to sign and panic ensued.

Bank accounts were emptied, bills jars were raided, sofas were turned upside down and elderly relatives were threatened. If Peter came home you would not be able to get in the ground and many people just abandoned work to rush to the ticket office with the contents of their children's freshly smashed piggy bank in one hand and the money for next week's food in the other. There was a large, frantic and excited queue up at SJP.

By the time we got back to work the radio people were back-pedalling like crazy. Peter was still in Spain with Everton and denied all knowledge while Newcastle United FC kept an inscrutable silence.

At the time we felt completely cheated, we had been deceived into buying season tickets that we didn't want and couldn't afford - now it seems like one of the wisest things we ever did.

CHAPTER 5

The Kevin Keegan Guide To Buying Players

History gets re-written in football on a season by season basis. Lazy and malicious journalists repeat the same old shit long enough for it to become the "Accepted Wisdom" and it gets repeated back at you by dimwits for the rest of your life.

For example: "Newcastle United used to be rubbish and were getting crowds of less than 15,000 until popular local philanthropist John Hall turned up and gave Kevin Keegan stacks of cash in a great big wheelbarrow and Newcastle bought their way from the bottom of the second division to the Premier League. In The Premiership Keegan took his spending to in excess of £70 million and was 20 points clear of Manchester United before going mad on live television, losing the title and walking out". - accepted wisdom.

All bollocks - not true - lies - utter bollocks. If you believe any of it you're wrong. You're wrong. You're wrong.

Truth is early on Kev was very frugal on strictly limited resources and his choice of new players was on the whole impeccable. Yes there was Darren McDonough and Peter Garland (who? - exactly) but KK was later happy to blame certain players' arrivals when he first came to the club on faulty recommendations by other people. This seems a little less than magnanimous but from the summer of 92, when Keegan accepts full responsibility, Newcastle constantly operated on a policy of only buying players who are better than the ones we'd already got. This seems childishly straightforward but most clubs can't manage it.

Keegan's eye for a player isn't up for question - except for goalkeepers. He doesn't know a good goalkeeper from a hole in the ground, spent a considerable amount of time, money and heartache on the problem and still Newcastle's best goalkeeper the day he walked out, Pavel Srnicek, was one who was here when he arrived. He did try to solve the problem by bringing in

Peter Bonetti as goalkeeping coach at one point. Bonetti was known as "The Cat" during his playing career but as this turned out to be less to do with any agile goalkeeping expertise and more about the probability that he used to shit in his neighbour's garden. He didn't stay long.

The press, local and national, eagerly threw up names of players bound for Newcastle many of which caused ripples of excitement, until the name of David Speedie was tossed into the ring. At the time Speedie was Newcastle fans' arch nemesis - documentary proof exists in 'The Mag's' end of season poll from 91/92 when he won an unprecedented majority in the "Most Annoying Player" category.

The level of bad feeling was already running high against the player before we went to Blackburn in Keegan's second game as manager. I personally timed his first dive at 40 seconds. Naturally he went on to score three goals, celebrating the third by swinging on the net like a poisonous little monkey and sticking his two fingers up at the Newcastle fans behind the goal. The rush to get at him caused a major disturbance and while the police and stewards struggled to maintain order the referee gently escorted him away.

Nearly caused a riot and all he got was a smile and a pat on the bottom from the ref. Granted, having 5-6,000 people singing, "We've all shagged your wife -Speedie Speedie", might be considered provocative but he annoyed us first. Damn it.

Still "Speedie For Toon" headlines caused outrage and the following conversation: "If that little bastard signs I'm not fuckin' goin any more. That's it finished."

"At least we get to boo him every week."

"We might like him if he played for us."

"Do you think his wife will come?"

Speedie, like most of the names plucked out of the sky, never arrived, thank the Lord.

Keegan's buying policy was actually massively refreshing. He wouldn't give anything away, he'd say nothing and just let the speculation blow about in the wind until BAM!

New Player. BAM -Venison. BAM - Beresford BAM - Bracewell.

Two full backs and a defensive midfielder was hardly stuff to get the pulse racing but Keegan's most important signing made us all sit up and feel the first prickle that something special was in the offing.

Bearing in mind that we had just avoided relegation to Division 2 and that Middlesbrough had been promoted to the shiny new Premier League the imminent move from Tyne to Tees of our Player Of The Season Mr Gavin Peacock was sad but understandable.

Then Gavin turned up on the local news (in a truly revolting tie) to announce that he'd signed a new contract with us and had been convinced that Newcastle United was a team going places. Good God! What did Keegan say to him?

We played Middlesbrough in a rare St James's Park pre-season friendly (in a tournament which included Real Sociedad and Bobby Robson's Sporting Lisbon), passed them virtually to death and Peacock scored the only goal. A penalty in front of the Middlesbrough fans who had spent the afternoon booing him. He didn't see the need then, or at any other point, to stick up his fingers at his detractors. That's our job.

CHAPTER 6

Optimism Or Self-Delusion

Football fans are a very cynical breed. They might start out all bright-eyed and eager but they very soon become distrustful and suspicious. It's only natural of course when absolutely everybody lies to you all the bastard time. Players tell you they love you and kiss the club badge on their shirts then 6 months later they are playing for somebody else. Managers and Chairmen are so nervous of getting an angry mob on their back that they will say just about anything to keep us sedated and the media has got more bollocks in it than a busy vet's dustbin.

As fans of Newcastle United we are used to a regular diet of disappointment and humiliation. We have also witnessed more false dawns than the judges at last year's International French & Saunders lookalike competition.

So why the hell we approach the start of every season like giggling school girls, God above only knows. We dine out eagerly at the Restaurant Of Optimism and we wash down platefuls of Self-Delusion with cold beer over a table built of False Hopes. We whip ourselves into a frenzy and believe that this year our team will prove to be greater than the sum of their parts and that all those purchases of players who we had never heard of will turn out to be strokes of utter genius. Rough diamonds, bursting with skill, who can be cut into new heroes.

We went to Everton for a first game of a season, more years ago than I care to remember, convinced we were going to win the League. Mirandinha, John Robertson and John Hendrie had ensured we won every pre-season game at least 7-0 and with the ammunition provided by Ian ("The New Paul Gascoigne") Bogie we were going to slash through the opposition like a swashbuckling gang of black and white musketeers. We lost the game 4-0 and were relegated. Within a year all the above strikers were sold and poor Ian Bogie barely got a game.

Two years later Ossie Ardiles' dashing young blades would begin their inevitable rush out of Division Two by humiliating Charlton, who had temporarily set up home at Upton Park. The fact that the trip would involve me spending at least 12 hours of my birthday, sober, on a minger of a bus powered by a lone elastic band, which apparently had been reserved for only the most flatulent of fans could not temper my impending glee. We lost.

Yet here we were again marching up to St James's with only our shiny new season ticket books and the warm glow of a pint too many to protect us from the pounding rain, convinced we were about to enter a whole new era. Southend United were to be our first victims and their ritual humiliation would send out a message of intent that would reverberate throughout the land.

In the years since, Kevin Keegan's tactical knowledge has been rubbished, his ability under pressure on the big stage brought up for public questioning. But as a rabble rouser he is second to none. Not for him the "we'll take each game as it comes" trotted out by lesser men. He proclaimed that we were going for the title and he said it with such passion that the pubs in town were positively vibrating with enthusiasm. If this was World War One he would undoubtedly have got us all killed because players and fans were ready to storm the enemy stark naked if that's what he wanted. C'MON!!!!

The gates of our section in the Gallowgate were locked. We couldn't get in.

A rush of panic. A growing band of late arrivals brandished their season ticket booklets like the supporters of Chairman Mao but the police had locked this gate and said we could go to the opposite Leazes End and pay on the gate there. There was a roar from inside as the teams came out and fans felt that unique surge of blood to the temples you get when outside a football ground with the game underway. Police horses were brought in to force angry fans away from the locked gates as panic and the rage of injustice threatened to get ugly. A group of fans declared they would storm the directors' box in protest but a lone policeman read the situation for what it was, urgently radioed and we were escorted to the centre of the Gallowgate. Through the desperate queue and clickerty-clickerty through the turnstile.

In.

Breathe.

A fierce noise was coming from the crowd as we scrambled desperately up the steps, past the stinking toilets, turn run, turn run and - instant sensory overload!

It all hits you at once: the noise, the colour, the movement. The live sea of black and white, the ball flashing white across the lush green of the grass. Senses swirl. Hundreds of games before this and hundreds after and still you reel physically at the first game. Newcastle were attacking the Leazes End.

As we eased our way through the throng there was suddenly a spectacular Peacock scissor kick -. the whole end full of fans rolled onto the balls of their feet, twitched their heads a fraction forward and took a sharp breath. The shot rattled off the post - the breath is let out in a groan and heads and feet ease back. We ended up low down on the terrace looking at the game through the posts of the Gallowgate End goal and our view of the shot Bracewell hammered into the Southend net was spine-tinglingly perfect. We were right behind it as, struck from the edge of the area, it swerved violently into the top corner.

Newcastle were breathtaking; the speed and accuracy of the passing, the movement, the confidence. Our hands were red raw from clapping by half time, the fact that the rain was still clattering down was of no consequence and Newcastle were 2-0 up already.

The crowd jabbered excitedly through half time, the thrill was extraordinary, it was like a completely different game to what we'd been watching previously and it was intoxicating.

Southend got a scabby goal. Newcastle roared back at them and Lee Clark poked the ball through the keeper's legs for 3-1. Southend scored another and refused to roll over.

Then we got anxious. The cold rain had soaked through my thick jacket, through my clothes and was damp and unpleasant next to my crawling nervous skin. We held on.

My jacket hit the floor of the Dog And Parrot like a lead weight and the first pint sloshed down my coarse throat in seconds. The grumpy and the pessimistic pointed out we had only beaten Southend but we shouted them down, cursed their worthless hides and ordered more beer.

The T.V. pictures never did do justice to that Bracewell goal.

CHAPTER 7

The Sun Always Shines On TV

A tremendous amount of what football fans had previously taken for granted changed going into the 92/93 season.

The most important thing, on the surface at least, was the fact that the F.A. had taken over the running of the country's top division from the Football League. "The Big Five"; Manchester United, Liverpool, Everton, Arsenal and Spurs had been whining like sick little bitches for years over the allocation of TV revenue. Wanting all of it, basically, and threatening to break away and take all the best players with them.

They got their wish with the help of the F.A.'s professional toady, Graham Kelly. The actual structure of the game would remain the same - there had been a threat of no promotion or relegation from this new fancy pants Premier League but as the "Big Five" saw themselves in no real threat of demotion it didn't come to pass.

The real change as far as the fans were concerned was who had control of the TV rights.

Snooker used to be massively popular in the 1980's - but then so did Miami Vice, A Flock Of Seagulls, ra-ra skirts and A-Ha. Girls with too much blusher and boys dressed like Lord Byron, burgundy staypress trousers, The A-Team and Timmy Fuckin' Mallet - the decade that brought shame on the nation is generally best forgotten.

But to this day snooker tortures itself over the lost viewing figures, weeping alone in the dark, late night corners of the TV schedule about when they used to have characters in the game and how the whole nation watched Alex "Hurricane" Higgins cry.

Truth is, snooker got popular because there was fuck all else to watch. ITV had the rights to all the football and they made an absolute bollocks of it. They outbid the BBC for the rights and then they didn't know what to do with it.

Fuckin' clueless bastards didn't know they were sitting on a gold mine and they thought showing Liverpool live every other Sunday and "The Saint & Greavsie" (pair of tits that they were) would just about exhaust Johnny Public's limited interest.

Sky Television, which until they got the football had "The Simpsons" and absolutely nothing else worth watching, saw the potential and teamed up with the BBC. ITV were out on their ear.

The BBC got the highlights and that meant Match Of The Day was back and better with the goals from ALL the games in the top flight. Let us not forget that under ITV's idiot stewardship some games didn't have cameras at them, or if they did they didn't relay them to the audience. The only way you could guarantee seeing your side's goals was to catch the local news and that would mean sitting through five minutes of watching some crappy, council funded art group dancing around with their fuckin' pants on their heads before you got what seemed like 30 seconds' worth of goals and interviews.

The regions dealt with their football independently and in the North East that meant "The Back Page", The Tyne-Tees Television moveable Sunday feast generally fronted by Roger Tames. "The Back Page" was bounced around the schedule like a red-headed step-child between disinterested relatives. The time it was advertised on screen or in the paper meant very little and the schedule was reshuffled in a pointless and arbitrary fashion on a whim and at a moment's notice. If you could track it down it was a distinctly unsatisfactory experience - badly made and never offering any real feel for the games. "The Back Page" was a shoddy bastard of a show but nevertheless essential viewing which meant fans wishing to at least re-live the goals they had previously only witnessed through a drunken haze could expect up to an hour of gardening programmes before Roger got to beam himself into their front rooms.

Sky showed games live and from the beginning they knew what they were doing and they did it well. There was the odd mistake, brought on perhaps by a lack of confidence that the paying public would still turn up to provide the atmosphere the armchair fan would require, so they provided dancing girls, firework shows and pop stars poncing about in the rain. The Shamen doing "Ebenezer Goode" in front of a disinterested Highbury is the stuff of TV legend as is a "happy" Mick Summerbee, on to offer expert analysis, claiming that his and his son's England careers were being sabotaged by some shadowy media conspiracy.

You needed to get a satellite dish installed and that cost money and many fans, myself included, chose not to bother. After all, what were we missing? Wimbledon, Crystal Palace, Sheffield United, Nottingham Forest, Sheffield Wednesday, Oldham. The two best footballing sides in the Division were Norwich City and Queens Park Rangers, Arsenal were a long ball team, Liverpool were a bloody mess and everybody else was rubbish except Man Utd and Aston Villa who just about managed to keep their faces out of the quagmire. (It's no wonder Sky welcomed Newcastle with such open arms - we actually gave them something worth looking at.)

Non-satellite viewers could see as much of the Premiership as we needed to on BBC1 on a Saturday night and instead of Liverpool painfully trying to strangle the life out of some poor saps on a Sunday afternoon we suddenly had Channel 4 showing Serie A football live from Italy with AC Milan , Juventus, Sampdoria and Roma - how exotic and exciting - and having to physically peel Wifey off the screen whenever Roma captain Guiseppe Giannini appeared was a side effect I, for one, could just about live with.

The other three English divisions were of no interest to the owners of this brave new world and they would have to deal with ITV as best they could. So Newcastle would not be on Sky, which meant for the most part you had an afternoon of tips on eradicating slugs whilst in search of "The Back Page", or you had to sit patiently through the local news. A couple of murders, a school in danger of closing, an old fella with a twenty year old pigeon who was going to be best man at his wedding until it laid a fuckin' egg and, lo and behold, five minutes of a council funded art group dancing around with their bastard pants on their stupid heads. Then 30 seconds of ITV camera work - which explains why the coverage of Bracewell's goal against Southend was all but missed.

Oh, and on the first weekend of The Premiership which game had the biggest attendance in the whole country? Why, if it wasn't Newcastle United versus Southend United. Richard Keys doesn't mention that too bloody often, does he?

CHAPTER 8

Happy Hours With The Family By The Wireless

Quite possibly the worst way to witness a football match is via the radio. The problem is you have senses to spare and that makes you fidgety. At a game your every fibre is consumed by the game. The sights, the sound, the smell combine so your feel for the game is absolute. I used to think I was always flat out fucked after a match because I was pissed - a rational explanation because I always was. Then having seen a couple of games sober I found I was still exhausted. Concentrating so intensely for the fat end of two hours, on each player's performance, the ref, the ball, the singing is bloody hard work.
TV, you lose a lot. You can't take in the big picture. Runs off the ball, players filling in gaps left by those out of position, it's all lost to you but despite not being able to feel the game you can at least see most of what is happening.
Radio, you are relying on one or two strangers' interpretation of what's going on and that is a recipe for mental torture. You have to find something else to do with your fidgeting mind and anything that takes any manner of concentration is a waste of time. Something along the line of alphabetising your record collection or bashing your head repeatedly off the wall is as good as you're going to manage. "Go to the fucking game then, you soft bastard," you may say. A good point well made and in an ideal world that would be fine. But this was a difficult time and getting into the habit of organising your life to be able to apply for tickets and organise travel arrangements was a new experience. For the majority of games turning up and paying at the turnstile was what everybody did. But allocations for away tickets were shrinking and you had to be quick off the mark and lucky.

Newcastle's surge to the top of the table had been slightly derailed because having had such a crappy season the year before we had to suffer the ignominy of playing in the first round of the League Cup. This meant that while we were struggling past Mansfield our rivals were playing and winning League games. To make matters worse, our next League game was away to Championship favourites Derby County.

The previous year over 6,000 of us had rattled the old Baseball Ground to its foundations, screaming at the injustice of a 4-1 defeat hastened by a rookie ref sending off three of our players and Terry McDermott. That was possibly the worst performance by a referee and the best performance by a travelling support I'd seen. The ref simply lost it and the crowd did brilliantly - firstly by not invading the pitch and skinning the bastard alive but mostly for the relentless wall of noise that had a tearful David Kelly throwing his shirt into the crowd at the end. The tickets were snapped up for the re-match in a flash, we missed out and were left with no option but Metro Radio and Mr Charles Harrison.

Our nephew came to visit, he was about 13 and had no interest in football. We took him to St James's Park when he was a lot younger, it was freezing cold and the game finished 0-0 with Oxford. I feel we may have scarred the lad for life. Football was a different world to him.
We were playing a board game with loads of bits all over the table and the radio on and Charles Harrison was doing his whole routine... "There's a chance on here......"
"To who, to who," we whooped like excited owls, do we wish for a goal or a save? Damn it.
"Newcastle look like they have weathered the storm," usually meant you had about a minute before we conceded a goal but "Oh dear, Tommy Wright will have to be quick here" meant our keeper had time to scratch his arse and do a little dance before collecting the ball comfortably.
At the board game Nephew was happily slashing his way through battalions of goblins and ogres while we, our minds 90% on the radio, died at the mercy of The Three Legged Hamster Monster or whatever it was...... then Newcastle scored and the bits all went flying up in the air.
In retrospect I understand the Nephew had never seen supposed adults behaving like we did. Jumping around hugging each other, running along the sofa and high-fiving whilst screaming and shouting. He looked at us with a kind of appalled amusement and his expression was the same when Newcastle made it 2-0. I remember he jumped when we both punched the table when Derby got one back and I have no idea what he was doing during the last five minutes as I was crawling around on all fours with my head in a cushion whimpering, "shut up, shut up, shut up, you fucker" as Charles Harrison said, "It looks like Newcastle have weathered the storm". It was, and remains, a wretched way to experience the football. Sometimes I won't even put myself through it any more- the lads at the match said we pissed it.

CHAPTER 9

Revenge Is A Dish Best Served Red Hot

Good drama needs quality villains, a hate figure to counter-balance the heroic and the good. Sherlock Holmes needs Moriarty and Spiderman needs the Green Goblin or you've only got half a story. "Sherlock Holmes Crosses Wits With Pongo the Binman" or "Spiderman Battles His Tax Returns" wouldn't hold your attention. A football team needs to be at war with Man Utd, Bayern Munich or Galatasaray.

You can tell that Newcastle had been too long out of the top flight by a glance at 'The Mag's end of season poll for 91/92: "Most Annoying Team" First Place: Cambridge United.

Fucking Cambridge, what Division are they in now?

God knows, but we actually used to let them bother us. And with good reason too. Their manager John Beck had spawned some kind of evil anti-football football team complete with loads of ghastly underhand tricks to irritate the opposition. Word has it that they gave the away team light balls to practise with then used heavy ones in the game. They lumped it long and pressed the ball. Yellow marks were painted on the corners of their ground's stands for the players to aim at, to get the ball into the corners. These corners were heavily sanded to hold the ball up for their wide men to run onto and bash crosses in for giant strikers. They were violent, mean-spirited and fundamentally nasty - in short quality villains. But the point remains if your arch nemesis is Cambridge bloody United then your sights are too low.

We had been kicking around with the dregs for long enough to have other enemies: players and teams who had wronged us. As football fans it is part of our make-up to bear grudges and part of the game's beauty that opportunities to right wrongs come round reasonably regularly.

The team of 92/93 was like a great big fucking black and white juggernaut of justice powered by beautiful but deadly angels intent on brutal revenge and we ran our enemies down like the diseased pigs they were. The Gallowgate crowd, filled with a lust for blood, gloated over the remains of teams shredded by our dynamic and relentless style.

("Our football is very aggressive. But we are not kicking people and hoofing balls in, we're actually mentally hurting them with the football we're playing," - Kevin Keegan).

A pattern developed where we bewildered a team with our speed of thought and movement, swarming all over them, scoring, then scoring again. BANG! no pause for breath BANG!. Sides would be clinging on for 0-0 at half time and before they knew it, it was 2-0. West Ham, BANG BANG 2-0. Former Hammer David Kelly responded to the abuse of the West Ham fans by scoring then pulling on the bottom of his shirt and screaming in front of them. And oh the joy at seeing Julian Dicks sent off. Always he seemed to get away with his special brand of ultra-violence but Franz Carr tortured the swine with his pace and trickery, Dicks eventually lost his rag and elbowed Carr in the face with the ref as closest witness. Bye Bye.

Every football fan in the country still bore a grudge against Luton. Even after they stopped banning away fans, dug up their plastic pitch, got rid of the despicable Tory MP chairman David Evans (who had so arrogantly shouted down the club's detractors) and transferred the odious head-banded Steve Foster. The hatred still burned.

In truth we had already extracted our revenge, returning a 4-0 thumping on the plastic with a 4-0 reverse at St James's, complete with ball juggling from Paul Gascoigne and Kenny Wharton famously sitting on the ball. Also two seasons previously they had amassed just enough points to relegate sunderland from their unrightful place in the top League. But this was no time for leniency. They hung on until just before half time then BANG BANG! 2-0 (Kelly & Clark).

We scrambled a 2-1 win on a tight bumpy pitch at Bristol Rovers thanks to Sheedy scoring from an 8 yard freekick courtesy of the new backpass law, David Kelly's belief in the lost causes, (keeping an impossible ball in and releasing O'Brien) and most importantly from the acrobatics of keeper Tommy Wright who made some of the best saves ever witnessed by man or indeed beast.

Portsmouth had to be punished at St James Park for being so damn far away (bastards) with The Toon 2-0 up by half time and running out 3-1 winners thanks to two goals from the new slimline Mickey Quinn who had been an unused substitute until that point, despite ridding himself of the wobbly man-tits.

Played six - won six. Our main rivals Charlton had played a game more, including a win at sunderland where mackem John Kay was sent off after a headbutt (something we don't see much of these days) and the home side scored two own goals (something you can never see enough of). But a Charlton home draw with the now slightly less evil Cambridge United meant Newcastle went top for the first time. It was such a big deal that most of us woke up on a floor the next day and 'The Mag' printed the League table as its front cover. Ha!

CHAPTER 10

The Backpass Law

The 1992/93 season was the first year that goalkeepers were forbidden to pick up kicked backpasses. Like so much else that has changed we all take it for granted now but at the time it was seen as being a big deal. Truth was it wasn't a big deal........

It was a bloody massive deal and it fundamentally changed football forever and for the better. I don't know whose idea it was but the person or persons responsible deserve free drink as well as streets, roses and pets named after them across the civilised world.

At first there was a period of utter anarchy. Hilarious chaos, It's A Knockout style clumsiness and buffoonery - injured goalkeepers and red-faced defenders. On the first day of the season Tony Adams of Arsenal (at this time still considered a comedy beast of burden rather than the established international defender of high repute he became) got hopelessly confused, trod on the ball, fell over and gifted Norwich City a goal. Across the country fans howled with glee.

The established order hated it and so did previously mollycoddled goalkeepers; normal fans lapped it up like dogs at spilt beer. Terry Venables and Alan Hansen on Match Of The Day complained that the players couldn't cope with the rule, like unco-ordinated and stupid defenders kicking desperate clearances into each others faces and crashing into one another in a state of blind panic was a bad thing. David Pleat moaned that the rule encouraged the longball game which was a statement that proved utterly false.

In a survey carried out by the Today newspaper (R.I.P- Rot In Pieces) 57% of Premiership goalkeepers polled were against the rule.

Garth Crooks, of all people, called it right, saying defenders and goalkeepers were being forced to think. The fact that this was something clearly beyond a good number of them only made for more entertainment.

Before the rule change, for years teams like Liverpool and Arsenal had strangled the life out of games by destroying the opposition's momentum with constant backpasses to their keepers. Going a goal down to teams like this at home was to encounter a game of soul-grating frustration. Teams like Wimbledon and Cambridge used their goalkeepers to drop-kick longballs as far and high up the pitch as possible for their big clumsy centre forwards to collide with, taking the percentage chance that it would bobble to another of their players. If not scramble it back and WUMPF! and scramble and WUMPF! and scramble. Serie A games in Italy where scores always seemed to be 0-0 or 1-0 were suddenly turning up with 5-3s.

Teams coming to Newcastle would consider the most important thing to do was quieten the crowd - this was best achieved through slowing the game down and ten backpasses to the goalkeeper in the first five minutes would set you well on the way. The tactic was to deliberately make the game less entertaining for the paying spectator so outlawing it was obviously a stroke of utter genius. The recognised longball teams Palace, Wimbledon, Southend, Cambridge and to a certain extent Arsenal immediately started struggling. The clever teams with actual footballers for goalkeepers and defenders flourished. Norwich and Queens Park Rangers in the Premiership and Newcastle United in the First Division with big bastard brass knobs on. West Ham and Swindon were worth watching as well.

The teams that didn't take the time or thought to come to terms with the backpass law looked like dimwitted clowns, the teams that did looked beautiful. Tommy Wright in the Newcastle goal comfortably and confidently fielded backpasses with his feet while the fullbacks had the sense to constantly pull wide and make themselves available to him. Moves developed from deep, the play was stretched and teams couldn't slow us down.

We were like a black and white whirlwind and teams were dizzied by us.

Former sunderland manager and expert-bellyacher Denis Smith arrived with his Bristol City side. In his own silly little world Smith's teams were never beaten by the better side - they were always hard done by. Bad luck or poor refs were the only things that could bring his teams down, we witnessed his whining for years on the local news as manager of sunderland and it wasn't surprising when he blamed weak refereeing after his side reaped the whirlwind and crashed 5-0. Like so many sides they survived until 5 minutes before half time when O'Brien hit a 25 yard free kick then Kelly was brought down for a penalty. A second penalty also knocked in by Peacock, a cute chip from Franz Carr and a belter from Brock saw off a clueless opposition. Bristol, missing the injured Andy Cole, were let off as our confidence hit new heights with brilliant passing and movement, excellent goals and one move in particular that saw three consecutive back-heels. As a mate, Bront, said in the pub afterwards, "We are going to give someone an absolute thrashing this season. And that wasn't it."

CHAPTER 11

Robert Lee

Newcastle had won their first 7 games by this point but Charlton were clinging to our leg like a randy terrier so it seemed mighty neighbourly of Middlesbrough to try to prise them off by spiriting away their best player. With little more than a passing interest from the Tyneside public, Robert Lee arrived on Teesside for talks and went home to think over a move that seemed straightforward. Newcastle pounced. Trouble is we had seen this sort of pouncing before - for example when Alan Shearer's move from Southampton to Blackburn was all but done, Newcastle reportedly came in with a late but smaller bid - God knows what we were trying to achieve but we kept doing it and the fans got sceptical. After all, the idea that a player would want to move from one team near the top of the First Division to another when he could go to a Premiership club seemed, quite frankly, daft. Turns out, according to the man's autobiography, Newcastle offered him less wages as well.

Less money and a Division lower. Yet somehow Keegan managed to shove Mr Lee into a wheelbarrow and rush him into a press conference (metaphorically, obviously) claiming he'd convinced the silly cockney that Newcastle was nearer than Middlesbrough to London.

The latter days of Rob's Newcastle career were somewhat blighted by Ruud Gullit trying to force him out the club; poor choices on his testimonial (bad timing, dull opposition and overpriced tickets compared to the Intertoto Cup games that took place either side of it) and eventually what felt like an untidy departure to Derby County BUT let it never be forgotten that Robert Lee was a prince at Newcastle. Sublime in quality and charming in temperament he was the best central midfielder in the country for four or five years and few Newcastle fans would have swapped him - even for Roy Keane. That is a nailed on fact and don't you forget it. Every summer the press would claim he wanted to go back to play and live in London and every year he came back laughing at the speculation.

Keegan said Bobby Lee was the best pound for pound player he ever bought and, self-effacing as ever, Lee claimed it was because he was so cheap but we got nine and a half years out of a player who in his prime could pass, tackle, shoot and sprint box to box forever. Cool under pressure, precise and professional at all times it breaks my heart when I think about how much stuff he deserved to win compared to how many gaudy pots he actually got to shake above his head. He says he's not bothered about the missed trophies and that he wouldn't have swapped his time at Newcastle for anything, which makes him a better man than me because every time I've seen some snivelling little shitpot or some whining bastard, or some fucker not fit to scrub out Robert Lee's fucking bins, holding a trophy that should have been ours, it grates against my living soul. I long ago came to terms with the fact that we're destined to win nothing, ever and enjoy myself accordingly - it simply doesn't seem fair on Robert Lee.

Newcastle United had probably 8 years, if not more, where we could not live without Lee. If he was missing or off his game we were a shadow of ourselves. He started on the wing but Keegan, who clearly adored the man, moved him inside to devastating effect. He earned the England caps that Keegan said were his for the taking and as the years got into his legs he had the brains to drop into a deeper defensive midfield role that was equally effective.

If you are a Newcastle fan then you know all this. None of this is news to you but sometimes we all forget the fact that Rob Lee has been the most important player to Newcastle United over these last ten (crazy-mental) years. Making more of an overall contribution than even Shearer, Cole or Beardsley.

And we shouldn't.

You should also remember that Robert Lee's Newcastle United debut, having chosen less money in a lower division, was at home. In the Coca Cola Cup - against Middlesbrough.

CHAPTER 12

...And Boro Of Course

Most football fans, and Newcastle fans in particular, have an attitude towards Middlesbrough and Middlesbrough fans that is deeply entrenched.

The place itself is uniquely, unarguably, unusually and spectacularly ugly: from miles away you can see the sprawling chemical plants and the monstrous chimneys belching shite into the sky and from up close much of the town matches the long-view. I can only describe the extremities of the hideousness by saying that I once had occasion to drive through Grangetown in Middlesbrough with somebody from sunderland who visibly shuddered - from sunderland for God's sake - can you imagine?

In the nation's subconscious the inhabitants of Middlesbrough are withered grey-skinned mutants who breathe their smog filled air through fish-like gills in the manner of some peculiar and grotesque land-fish. They live out their disappointing, unfulfilling and ultimately short lives in filthy hovels where they devour their own young and rarely see a nutritious breakfast. Many of them have two heads.

Middlesbrough FC have never achieved anything, even in the baggy-shorted black and white filmed days when, for flip's sake, even Newcastle United found silverware a breeze. Instead they are doomed to veer violently through the Divisions like a drunk driver in an American ''Police Stop'' video. Because of this most football fans, and Newcastle fans in particular, never take Boro seriously and look down their noses at them even if they are playing in a higher Division (an impressively gymnastic feat) - thus Boro fans hate most football fans and Newcastle fans in particular.

Everybody takes the piss out of them. And all the time, which is why it's surprising that they are so extraordinarily easy to wind up. During the 1991/92 season the teams met at Ayresome Park during a campaign where an understrength Newcastle struggled to survive and Boro got promoted. The place is now a housing estate but it used to be a mutated farmyard with a football pitch in the middle. The main stand was a 3-sided abandoned warehouse, the stands behind the goals were seemingly barns that had fallen into hopeless disrepair while the remaining side appeared to be an abattoir for destroying diseased swine. The away section was a corner between the abattoir and one of the barns, concrete terrace about half of which afforded you a view of a pitch that your best players spent most of the game rolling around on. Boro had been extraordinarily violent for years but Lennie Lawrence had made them effective as well and they were 3-0 up with five minutes left.

The away allocation was previously 2,000 but Boro had cut this to 1,000 because a load of Leeds fans had spent a game popping out of the crowd like wet bars of soap because they had all squashed together with the unreasonable motive of trying to see the game. Because of the way tickets were allocated our 1,000 was made up mostly of comfortable trousered season ticket holders and junior travel club members, which meant noisewise we were slaughtered as well. The understrength Newcastle support should have been humbled and humiliated but with the Cleveland Sex Abuse scandal still fresh in the memory they began a chorus of, "Shag your bairns, shag your bairns, shag your bairns," and the locals simply flipped. Screaming unintelligible abuse through faces twisted with utter hatred. They waved their arms, stuck their fingers up, fought with stewards to get at us and .... we laughed and laughed and laughed.

Boro fans only seemed to have three songs; "Come on Boro" , "We hate Geordies and we hate Geordies" - like that was ever going to hurt our feelings - and "Middlesbrough.... by far the greatest team the world has ever seen" which was clearly a monumental lie brought on by the kind of self-delusion that made the Roman Emperor Caligula make his horse a senator and go to war against the sea.

With sunderland we always strive to exert our superiority, with Boro they can be in what ever Division the hell they like as long as it's different to ours and their promotion the previous season meant we didn't have to go there and we didn't have to put up with them or their silly songs.

WRONG.

Coca-Cola Cup - two legs - first at St James's. Dammit.

The gang of degenerates I drink with traditionally worked their way along

Percy Street pre-match. I can't remember why we didn't the night of the first leg but there was hell on. Ironically, along that stretch only days before there had been gangs of police marching up and down, menacing fans who thought it might be nice to take their drinks out of the crowded pub into the sunshine. Bye-laws were invoked, landlords were threatened and we were all squeezed back inside. This night as a gang of Boro fans rampaged along the same street smashing windows and hurling missiles the constabulary were apparently slightly less evident.

After the game (in which Rob Lee made a steady start and Newcastle thrashed Boro 0-0) retribution was drunkenly demanded until our mate Kev pointed out that who would notice if we smashed up Middlesbrough? What we should do is go down there and tidy the place up, do a bit of landscape gardening. Maybe build them a new hospital. They would be livid.

CHAPTER 13

The Bastard A1

All English teams are south of Newcastle - it's a geographical fact that we have to live with. Like we have to live with the fact that Newcastle fans have to travel further than anybody else if they want to take in away games. An Arsenal fan once had the fuckin' gall to complain to me that having Newcastle and sunderland in the same division as them was a tremendous inconvenience because it was such a long way for them to come. I was so stunned and appalled that I spat beer all over the floor.

So 9 times out of 10 if you drive it's the A1 and, honestly, I'm sick of the sight of the bastard. It's not so much travelling down; then you have excited chatter, anticipation, hope and an afternoon of beer and football stretched out in front of you. The real pain is coming back and that stretch between Wetherby and Scotch Corner where you seem to be travelling through some sort of space/time fault, where hours seem to pass and yet you are getting no nearer home.

It's all very well getting misty-eyed and romantic about coming home over The Tyne Bridge but at least part of that is relief at not being on the A fucking 1 anymore.

Legally football fans should be allowed to drive as fast as they like of course, we have places to be and duties to perform and it is not our fault if there have been roadworks or accidents or if we left an hour late because we were drinking to insensibility down the Quayside the night before.

Truth is the A1 is considerably better than it used to be (well at least southbound it is, north of Alnwick it's little more than a farm track but as we don't play Berwick Rangers very often, that is of little relevance here). But the years it took to upgrade were a bloody nightmare and while Newcastle United fans mobilising in the numbers they did when we went to Peterborough was an awesome sight to behold, you could almost hear the old road creaking under the strain.

We set off in plenty of time driving a hire car in the traditional fashion, with foot down and stereo up, soon leaving the grotty weather for scorching sunshine. Carmate Ian had brought a tape that he had made especially which was deliberately obscure and tuneless and initially quirky and amusing. He insisted one of the songs (an elderly gentleman groaning from inside a washing machine) was entitled "Blind Man's Penis" and the rest of the tape seemed to be Arabian pigs attempting to yodel while drunk people hit dustbins with little sticks.

The alternative was Dave Lee Travis on Radio One (Five Live was yet to spring to life with its dynamic pre-match build up which these days starts at about 3 in the morning).

As yodelling Arabian pigs was clearly the better option compared to "The Hairy Twatflake" we didn't get the traffic report that must have said, "For God's sake get off the A1, it's backed up for ten bloody miles and it's going to be a fucking nightmare".

We were sucked in like a hapless Sixties television cowboy in quicksand. We stopped.

We crawled. We stopped and the pigs yodelled on. We snapped at each other, second-guessed the problem, squirmed and snapped at each other some more. And it got hotter and those fuckin' pigs........

I got out and as far as the eye could see in both directions were two lanes of motionless cars surrounded by restless and infuriated black and white shirts. The police raced up and down the hard shoulder telling everybody to get back in their cars in case they were knocked down and a senior citizen in a Toon top politely suggested that the only thing likely to knock us down were police cars racing up and down the hard shoulder warning us about getting knocked down. We eventually crawled through the roadworks and naturally the road on the other side was virtually clear - the tape with the yodelling pigs was last seen clattering across the hard shoulder and honest to goodness balls-out industro-rock ("Longue Route" by The Young Gods if you are playing along at home) accompanied our desperate hurtle towards Peterborough. "C'MON!"

Peterborough must have wondered what the bloody hell had hit it as 8,000 Newcastle fans swarmed across the place like an invading army. The town was a mass of black and white and the pubs where the landlords hadn't put up shutters and hid under the table were doing a roaring trade until the police got jumpy and started closing them down. Point of interest here: when the police do this anywhere they never seem to bother with supermarkets and off-licences. The determined alcoholic is rarely defeated.

London Road, home of "The Posh", was a joy to behold - good old fashioned pay cash to get in, stand on a terrace, jump around, black and white, chaotic madness. We seemed to have half the ground and were kicking up such an unholy racket that the players of both teams seemed visibly stunned as they came out.

Ian Bennett played a great game in the Peterborough goal but the most notable thing from the game apart from Sheedy's well taken goal was the obvious quality of Robert Lee; you got that rare "oo, he's good and now he's ours" tingle reserved for players like Asprilla, Ginola, Robert and Dyer. The jump from "mmm maybe" to "WHOA YES!"

We slaughtered them 1-0 for 85 minutes and clung on desperately for the last five. Coming out of the ground into a beautiful sea of jubilant black and white was breathtaking. There were legions of us and in the sunshine we looked fantastic.

Of course it took an hour to get out of town and the A fuckin'1 was a nightmare but when you've won it's bearable. One more chorus of "Blind Man's Penis"? C'mon, you know the words!

CHAPTER 14

Blank Saturdays

Games that kick off at three o'clock on a Saturday are rare and precious things to be treasured in this day and age. The idea that teams could go for months without seeing the traditional starting time would have seemed like insanity ten years ago when Newcastle being live on the TV still gave you a tingle of excitement rather than a feeling of "Oh for fucksake not again?!" In the 92/93 season Newcastle United didn't have a Saturday without a match until the start of October. In the 02/03 season we didn't have a Saturday at home with a match until October the 5th.

Away to Brentford with the game beamed out live on ITV (but only in London and across the North East. Bizarre.)

Kevin Keegan, newly crowned Manager Of The Month, turned up on as a guest on Football Focus as the BBC finally admitted that there was life outside the Premier League. As ever, Keegan's performance was masterful laying his praise on for us fans with a great big bloody shovel that had the soppy amongst us tearful and the rest swelling with pride.

This was to be the time where Newcastle broke above ground - until then witnessing the blinding brilliance of our new team had been a strictly limited privilege - now millions had the chance to see what all the fuss was about and we could video the game and watch it again and again. No more relying on shoddy highlights to fill in the bits we'd missed or drunkenly forgotten.

The assembled mass in our living room peered from over a wall of beer and crisps indulging in the most pointless, yet satisfying, acts in the world: shouting at the television. A football fan's need to shout, sing and cheer (and in some cases bare his ample bottom) at a television remains one of the world's great unsolved mysteries and Newcastle fans are amongst the most guilty. And our attitude to commentators and co-commentators is like that of a mother towards her delinquent son. We are allowed to call our team worse than shite

but woe betide the unfortunate outsider who risks criticising our players.
Lennie Lawrence, possibly the most charming and sensible manager Middlesbrough had seen in years was in the hapless position of co-commentator; praising Newcastle was stating the bloody obvious and anything else was heresy and he would be showered with abuse and peanuts from behind the beer wall.

We could see the three thousand Newcastle fans jumping up and down and we could clearly see that they were singing their heads off but all we could hear was a dozen Brentford fans singing a song about hitting Keegan on the head with a baseball bat. At the time we angrily dismissed this as "cockney sabotage" but over the years it has become clear that ITV regard an atmosphere as a nuisance and that they mistakenly believe that the armchair fan would rather hear the wittering of fools above the passion of a mob in full voice.

The teams were just coming out when there was a knock at the door - we all looked at each other and shrugged - no one missing.

Jehovah's fuckin' Witness!

Jehovah's fuckin' Witness wandering round Newcastle banging on folks' doors with the Toon live on telly. "What are you laughing at?" he said, as the door banged shut in his face.

Twat.

A forceful wind and a clumsy Brenford did their level best to spoil the "Newcastle United Show" but after ten minutes the all-action David Kelly smashed in a chance from a narrow angle and the whole street knew about it. During the all too rare quiet and reflective moments we may cringe at our own behaviour (running up the street in my underpants when Ketsbaia scored in Zagreb being a painful personal ghost) but at the time nothing else is of any consequence in the whole wide world .

The game should have been a slaughter but the idiot linesman nearly dislocated his bastard shoulder in his eagerness to flag our clearly onside boys offside and the Roger Tames/ Lennie Lawrence combination was proving equally at odds with our thinking.

"There's no need for Scott to get involved there," compared to, "Go on Scotty son, knock his fuckin' head off."

Rob Lee turned in the box and banged a shot onto the bar and before we had a chance to finish a decent groan Peacock had dived in to head home the rebound.

"Game over," said Lawrence and we cursed his foolish gun-jumping then and when Brentford pulled one back. When in the second half he accused Lee Clark of diving after both his legs were kicked from under him during our third fruitless penalty claim the man's ears should have been virtually on fire as armchair Tyneside raged.

We survived one late scare to go five points clear in the League and the TV interviewed a breathless Gavin Peacock on the pitch: "With support like this away from home you can't help but do well," and from behind the battered ramparts of a once proud beer wall came a hearty cheer because we had been there in spirit.

CHAPTER 15

Boro Again

At the start of the classic movie "Bladerunner" a ship flies into a filthy futuristic city. Monstrous chimneys belch rancid clouds of noxious gases into its skies and it is clear from shot one that this is going to be a place full of thieves, rogues and whores who will cut your throat and leave you twitching in a skip as soon as look at you. It is traditional, at this point, for the North Eastern film buff to announce, "Look everybody, it's Middlesbrough" and everyone else will titter and guffaw. Then "Bladerunner" director Ridley Scott said in 2000 that the opening shot was indeed based on the Teesside skyline and everything changed. Instead of ridiculing the ugliness, you find the place becomes fascinating and on visiting, instead of enduring the hideousness, it's possible to imagine that you are, in fact, embarking on a perilous and exotic adventure. Middlesbrough may have more than its fair share of under-age prostitutes and dumb-fuck-heroin addicts and may lack sizzling noodle bars frequented by Harrison Ford but you feel like you're on another planet when you're there - and that's got to be exciting hasn't it?

The people turn out to be different to how you imagine as well. Boro fans in and around Newcastle used to be like good jokes at a funeral; there probably were some about but nobody ever mentioned them. Now as more people move further away in search of better work they seem to turn up quite regularly. I was personally guilty of thinking of Smoggies as pollution-mutated mackems but they are actually a different breed all together. For a start when did sunderland ever offer the world anybody like Boro-born comedian Bob Mortimer. Their humour is twisted, left field and occasionally very black.

Their intense hatred of sunderland is endearing too.

Like other football fans Boro supporters hate all other teams - fair enough, we've all got a job to do but what seems peculiar about Boro fans (apart from their funny voices) is the fact that they seem to really hate their own team as well. They rarely miss an opportunity to slaughter their own players, announce their uselessness to all who will listen and, most impressive of all, actually stop going to support them in massive numbers. A couple of shit seasons and their crowds evaporate into the smog-filled night.

And the song "Middlesbrough.... by far the greatest team the world has ever seen" which drove me nuts for years because it was so obviously untrue.........turns out that it's ironic. It's a self depreciating piss-take - well that knocked the wind right out of my sails.

Of course the real reason my dislike for Middlesbrough has faded over these last ten years might not have anything to do with some new enlightenment. It's probably that we really hated them because going up to that Coca Cola Cup game in 92 we hadn't won at Ayresome Park since 1964. They were an evil spirited bogey team and we couldn't exorcise their malignant influence. We knew we were better than them but our only living proof was the size of our crowds - recent results favoured them and they were, at this point, a Division higher but this tie established the facts cold and hard.

For a start Boro were 1,000 under their allocation for the 0-0 draw at SJP, we took over 6,000 down there and simply blew them out of the water. The Bogey Man had his head cut clean off and we danced on the corpse until late into the night.

The sky was an unearthly purple as we approached Middlesbrough, for the first time we forsook the relative safety of the supporters' buses and went by car. While this meant skulking through the filthy labyrinth of backstreets around Ayresome Park we actually got to see the kick off. The people who had come on the official buses, again, for the most part filtered in late. To this day the Teesside Police stop the buses on the A19, keep you there until two minutes to kick off then escort you in to undermanned turnstiles. People who travel by coach to Middlesbrough have never, ever seen the kick off. Fact.

On this purple tinged night our noise was fearsome - after years of being hopelessly outnumbered the competition rules had granted us decent support and it was serious payback time and while singing "Down on your daughters, you're going down on your daughters" might have been considered a little unpleasant it made us laugh through our nervousness.

The first game had been competitive but Boro seemed determined to make this one a war. O'Brien was viciously hacked at early on and he did well to stay on his feet. He went down under a harder challenge and got up and grabbed his assailant by the neck. Clearly our players were keen to put up a decent fight as well. Cool.

Lee Clark was brought to ground again and again: he was pushed, jostled and kicked. They tackled him brutally, late and with little punishment in return. Hendrie tried to tear Beresford in half with a high tackle and eventually there was a booking. Beresford was quickly booked for exacting his own justice and it became clear that this time we were not going to be intimidated.

The Geordies in the crowd were of similar opinion and from where we were standing it seemed that every chorus of "Come on Boro, come on Boro" was crushed under the mighty juggernaut of our "Fuck off Boro, Fuck off Boro!"

Just before half-time David Kelly raced through a dithering defence to chest down and rifle home the ball to screaming pandemonium from the mass of black and white behind the goal.

Wilkinson's equaliser for Boro only seemed to fire us up more.

Clarkie was taking longer to get up after each assault but the arrival of Mick Quinn gave us a lift because him and the Boro crowd shared a mutual contempt that fuelled our fire.

Then move of the match - Howey moving towards his own goal, seemingly under pressure calmly knocked the ball out to Beresford who moved up the wing until he fed Clark who cut in and shot. The shot was blocked but Peacock was onto it and fed Quinn who moved it into the path of O'Brien who drilled a low shot into the corner of the Boro net. Boro tried to come back at us but after comfortably swatting aside their resistance Rob Lee and Clark combined to cross for Kelly who (after one of those dizzying moments where time stands still) swept the ball in for 3-1.

The Bogey Man was dead. And now it was time to dismember the corpse and send his widow a corsage.

Tommy Wright turned to us with his arms up, Bez ran towards us with his fists clenched while all our other players piled onto Kelly who on the final whistle ran the length of the pitch to throw himself on the ground in front of us. Quinn raised a triumphant fist at the Boro fans in the Holgate End while Keegan waved as we chanted his name. Team and fans were one. It was beautiful and we were exaltant.

Outside the scenes were crazy with car horns blasting and kids hanging out of windows screaming their jubilation. The traffic was a chaotic mess of waving scarves, blasting radios and wild-eyed glory.

Back home we eagerly awaited the match highlights on TV, only to witness a game that didn't reflect the dominance of Newcastle, that we had seen with our own eyes ('The Mag' ran a piece about how the Iraqis nearly nicked a draw out of the Gulf War - if Tyne Tees had done the coverage). Most of the dodgy tackles were edited out too but Lennie Lawrence's magnanimous "we were outplayed completely" restored our good cheer.

We went to Chelsea in the next round and lost 1-2. But in the greater scheme of things it was probably for the best; we already had a hell of a lot of games to play and the legacy from that night lasted a long time. The spell was broken and so was Boro's flimsy argument about being the region's top team. In the ten years since, Newcastle have slapped Boro stupid often enough and our ground now dwarfs theirs to such an extent that the argument seems silly, even to them, and that one purple-skied night had gone a long way to setting everything straight.

CHAPTER 16

Going To sunderland

The brutal truth is that Newcastle fans don't need to go to sunderland for anything except the football. In fact except for the football, nobody needs to go to sunderland. Ever. There is nothing there of any importance or interest. In a recent newspaper travel feature a woman complained that arriving in sunderland she couldn't find a hotel. That's because there is no demand - who would stay in them? Tramps and the certifiably crackers maybe, but can they afford room service?

Mackems wandering around The MetroCentre, Eldon Square or Newcastle Airport in sunderland gear may think they're being provocative or funny but they are actually merely highlighting that they haven't got any decent shops and that the Wright brothers' finest invention has somehow passed them by. If they want to catch a mainline train they have to come to Newcastle.

In 1992 there was a cinema in sunderland but no cathedral. Now the cinema is closed and they still haven't got a cathedral but they insist on being referred to as a city. No cinema in a city; how fuckin' backward is that?

sunderland's only claim to being a city is the size of its population and it is a larger place than most imagine but surely this has something to do with not understanding how contraception works and the fact that they are too inbred and pig-ignorant to think about living somewhere half decent.

Unlike Middlesbrough, sunderland do qualify for some sort of Green Environmental Award due to the entire place being run on hot air. One day enough of them are going to realise this and their cushion of self-delusion will burst and blow the whole sorry lot of the fuckers into the North Sea.

Football-wise sunderland AFC (the "A" is preposterous incidentally) are a long ball team traditionally. They have lumped it long and scrapped for the bits for as long as any living person can remember. They are lucky as well but that's because they are in league with the Devil and he looks after his own. They seem perpetually blessed with favourable refs, understrength opposition, a ball that spins and bounces bizarrely in their direction and just when you think you've got them in your sights and now we've got you, you slippery bastards, the weather will go insane - winds will blow up to 80 miles an hour or there will be a monsoon and biblical flooding. They are intrinsically evil and must be destroyed.

In 1990 Newcastle finished 3rd, sunderland 6th. They beat us in the play off semi-final fair and square. BUT they lost to Swindon in the final. Swindon were found guilty of financial irregularities and (unlike Tottenham who were also found guilty of a similar charge) were immediately relegated a Division. Who should get their place? Newcastle finished highest but we had lost to sunderland. Blackburn had more points than sunderland and had also lost to Swindon (in the semi-final). If Swindon had been busted earlier West Ham would have made the play-offs so they had cause for complaint as did Sheffield Wednesday who had been relegated from the First Division for finishing 3rd bottom.
The League chose sunderland and they would have got away with it too except they were bollocks and were immediately relegated after just one season.
In contrast Newcastle hit rock bottom and had to be re-built from scratch. If we had got promoted in 1990 we wouldn't have ever been desperate enough to take the road we did take which would have meant no Keegan. The forces of darkness may have given sunderland a hand but in the end they set off a chain of events that we wouldn't have swapped for the world. In short, like when they beat us in the rain on an unplayable pitch to finally see off Mad Ruud Gullit, by beating us they had done us a favour.

In 1992, however, the gulf between the two sides was so massive that even the Prince Of Lies, Beelzebub himself couldn't save their worthless souls. Keegan's blessed Hurricane Of Revenge was in town and the Horned One must have been doing a bit of shopping at The MetroCentre.

October 18th 1992 and the previous weekend Newcastle had warmed up for the derby with a 1-0 win over Tranmere. Our tenth League victory in a row. sunderland, under the expert guidance of manager Malcolm (Willy Wonka)

Crosby, live on television, had crashed and burnt spectacularly 6-0 at West Ham. As was traditional at the time, the kick-off was 12 noon on a Sunday as the police publicly admitted their embarrassing inability to control a relatively small crowd (compared to Glasgow, Manchester or Liverpool) as well as their ignorance in underestimating our need for (and imagination for getting) a lot of strong booze down our necks before the kick off. We had around eight and a half thousand fans in Roker Park and most of them had had a drink. sunderland, shamefully, had not sold out their tickets, which rank cowardice invited over-eager Geordies into the spaces left. The police outside told us that they believed around three thousand fans in sunderland areas of the ground were probably from Newcastle and their plan was basically to hope for the best.

The tension was hideous. We couldn't have them of all people spoiling our 100% record and our belief in our own team's superiority was small comfort with the impending chaotic lottery of a non-football match. Derby games are always ugly, bloody and unpleasant - the footballing equivalent of trench warfare.

The first audible volleys of abuse began. We jingled our keys and sang, "You've got Willie Willie Willie Willie Wonka on the bench" while the slack-jawed gawping half-breeds grunted back at us.

Then a fan jumped onto the pitch out of the Newcastle end and ran towards one of the discarded practice balls - we roared him on as stewards scampered after him. He was too swift for them and dribbled the ball the length of the pitch before lashing it into the goal at the Fulwell End, briefly celebrating before surrendering to the nearest steward.

"1-0, 1-0, 1-0," we sang.

The teams were due to come out and as usual that was the cue for the first in-ground fights to break out in the paddocks over to our left.

Order restored, the teams took the field and with little ceremony we were into it. As ever sunderland came out clattering everything that moved, yet somehow winning more free-kicks. Like at Boro, Lee Clark was clearly in for a bruising 90 minutes but the lad never lacked bravery and, rarely for a derby, we were seeing something resembling proper football. Gavin Peacock got the ball with his back to goal and jack-knifed a pass out to Robert Lee who was bursting forward. His cross went into a flurry of arms and legs and the ball somehow ended up in the sunderland goal. Owers had tackled Brock and scored an own goal but nobody in the black and white explosion in the Roker End seemed to know that. Fights broke out all over the rest of the ground as jubilant Mags blew their cover. The game was delayed and order was restored with some fans being ejected and some wedged in with the rest of us. In the meantime the lad who had jumped onto the pitch and scored the goal had somehow got back in the ground and was being chaired around shoulder high by the cheering mob. sunderland pushed for an equaliser and this recklessness suddenly presented David Kelly with a chance to make it 2-0. He tried to take the net out but dragged his chance wide.

A generous ref was awarding an unnatural amount of free kicks to the home side around our area and this fuelled our nervous aggravation although our team seemed remarkably calm. Owers poked a dreadful free kick straight at the Newcastle wall but seconds after we'd cheered our relief the ref booked Beresford for encroaching and let Owers take it again; this time he clipped the bar. Another soft free kick awarded after sunderland's Peter Davenport tripped over his own stupid feet resulted in Gary Bennett scoring but the ref had seen the push and disallowed it.

In the second half we continued to defend competently until the whiff of sulphur that led to the introduction of the odious Gordon Armstrong, whose scuffed shot deflected off a cloven hoof and past Tommy Wright for 1-1 and the nightmare sight of a celebrating Roker Park.

The mackems to our right, who always seemed to be looking at us and not the pitch, gloated, "Where's your record gone?" We jingled our keys "What's it like to be outclassed?" And I swear thousands of Mags looked at them, looked at the pitch, looked back at them and burst into spontaneous laughter.

On the pitch our lads calmly reasserted themselves until eventually David Kelly was hacked down on the edge of the area and we got "Liam O'Brien's Free Kick". One of the most magnificent and legendary goals in Newcastle United's history. Time went so slowly it hurt. The shuffling wall, the heart in mouth waiting.

O'Brien stepped up and struck it up and over the wall. And we just had time to think, "it must be going well over the bar because the keeper has never moved." It flew into the top corner and was suddenly bouncing in the net before anybody but O'Brien realised and he was already racing away, arms wide in celebration.

The speed, shock and brilliance of the goal seemed to catch a lot of people out. There was an excellent picture in The Journal on the Monday which showed the ball still bouncing in the net, O'Brien turning away and some of his team mates are stock still. But it's in the crowd that you can see people in different stages of celebration. Some jumping up, some mouth open and some yet to comprehend. Within seconds it was mass hysteria. With no thought to personal safety people were leaping all over each other, tumbling down the terrace, colliding with barriers and screaming their euphoria to the heavens.

The ref began to give more and more weird free-kicks to sunderland around our area: Tommy Wright for over-stepping the 18 yard line, Lee Clark for being flattened.

Newcastle had chances to put the game to bed, a Peacock chip, a Clark inswinger but the cushion we fans desperately needed wouldn't come. Our players' assurance was in stark contrast to our lack of it and Robert Lee turning majestically and passing out of trouble when we were all frantic for a desperate boot clear underlined the difference in attitude.

We finished the game by winning three consecutive corners, on the second a lad shouted "Howay man ref, how long left?" The ref looked, raised one finger and smiled.

A minute later our players who had been the picture of calm were leaping all over each other, shouting and punching the air as the final whistle blew. As usual many mackems chose to stand around staring at us rather than going to the pub like normal people - stupid fuckers.

Ten years on and experience has taught me to hold my nerve. Panicking doesn't help, it's bad for your health and more importantly it's bad for your team. I've convinced myself that the butterflies are excitement not fear: do your job, support your team and leave the rest to them. You don't have to go any less mental when we score or on the final whistle when we've won. You don't have to drink any less beer beforehand or when you get back to civilisation. And as I looked through the net at the Stadium of Light as Nicos Dabizas headed in the winner in the 2002 derby I knew as I did in 92 that the only place I wanted to be on the whole planet at that point was sunderland - and how often does anybody get to say that?

CHAPTER 17

When The Wheels Come Spinning Off

When Newcastle played Tranmere the week before the sunderland match, season ticket holders had the quality bars of Percy Street virtually to themselves. You could get a seat if you wanted, swift service at the bar and, theoretically at least, room to swing a number of cats (The 1992 Three Bulls Heads' All England Cat Swinging Competition never got off the ground).

A friend who had to work some Saturdays and was always skint anyway and thus season ticketless left at 1.30 to queue up at the ground and as the rest of us stumbled up at five to three he was disconsolately walking away among the estimated 8,000 who had been locked out. The press and the club love stuff like that but many among that 8,000 had watched too much piss poor football in too much bad weather for too many years for it to seem fair.

Strangely enough, there had never been so much elbow room on the terraces but the Taylor Report and safety worries meant numbers were strictly limited in the ground and it made for bad feeling. People started eyeing what they considered unfamiliar faces suspiciously.

Fans were more aggressive and argumentative and as usual, some people were starting to talk a lot of shit. "We need to lose a couple of games to get rid of some of these fucking strangers!" which was stupid enough but the bloke who said it was among regulars in the season ticketed area.

Newcastle won but were less than their scintillating best. People trudged away like we had lost and the post match analysis in some of the pubs was pointlessly hostile.

Coming into the Grimsby match Newcastle hadn't lost for 20 games. The wins at Boro and sunderland were such highs that it took too much effort to get excited about bloody Grimsby. The day after thinking "How can life possibly get any better than this" can be a harsh and depressing day. Three days after

Newcastle beat Manchester United 5-0 in 96/97 we went to the ground to face Oldham knowing that even if we won 20-0 it wouldn't be the same and the ground was a morgue.

We'd gone up like a rocket and the rush was magnificent but for some reason we looked down and the pressure was mounting.

Like when we were 12 points clear of Man Utd in 95/96, the lead becomes a burden. You get paranoid because you can feel the media and your enemies wanting you to fail, to unravel in front of them and it's desperate.

Newcastle fans are brilliant underdogs, we get drunk and take the piss out of ourselves and it's all a big laugh. When it comes to winning stuff the passion turns to fear for too many of the fans. I heard more than one person suggest it would have been better to have lost to Tranmere so sunderland couldn't stop our winning run - work that out.

Grimsby beat us 1-0 with a last minute goal. Audible booing was heard.

We next went to nasty Stamford Bridge with 6,000 fans, the old fashioned half a mile away from the pitch. The crowd was 30,000+ (9,000 more than Premiership Chelsea's highest attendance of the season thus far) and we lost 2-1 with big stupid ugly Mick Harford scoring the winner. Chelsea may ponce around in their fancy trousers these days but then they were a gobshite-ugly-cockney-long ball team, managed by Ian Porterfield and the following Saturday only 13,000 of them turned up for a League game.

By the time Newcastle lost a tight game 2-1 at Leicester the following Saturday that we easily could have won (even with Kevin Sheedy sent off) the media seemed to be turning on us and gloating. The hysteria was full blown. The pissy-knickered cowards were running around wailing and crying like Chicken Licken. "Keegan isn't a proven manager", "We need a big lad up front", "Robert Lee was a waste of money" "The defence is shit", "The sky is falling in".

Ten years on and have we learnt anything? The hysterical pissy-knickered little cowards will still boo good Newcastle teams off if they perceive they have under-performed. They will still slag off their own players and write stupid letters to the papers saying "The defence is shit", "Robert's lazy", "Shearer's past it", "The sky is falling in".

A sizeable proportion of our crowd have learnt fuck all - and it's depressing.

CHAPTER 18

I Am The Driver. I'm In Control

Rules For Travelling By Car:

Rule 1. The driver is a cross between God, Hitler and your Dad. He controls everything and you do as he says. Departure times, fuel breaks, bog stops, temperature, miles per hour, parking and music. No one else in the vehicle is allowed to touch anything without his express permission. The Driver creates all the rules and can choose to change them without complaint from other car members. If his expulsion of packets of Monster Munch on the grounds that "they smell funny" seems unfair - tough. Get out and walk if you don't like it. But as Spiderman says, "With great power comes great responsibility." And fuel, oil, sobriety and not crashing horribly and killing everybody are the driver's personal crosses which he must bear with a calm dignity.

Rule 2. The passenger seat, by order of manners, has to go to the partner of the driver. If the partner is not present this seat is reserved for the navigator. The post of navigator will be granted to the passenger with the most previous experience of the destination or failing that the gadgee with the longest legs. Preferably the navigator should not be female. Women may be generally more lovely, sensible and mature than men but they can't read maps and are likely to have an impromptu hissy-fit about you snapping at them if you demand information quickly, throwing the map or A to Z on the floor, folding their arms and pouting while the car drifts past exit ramps and aimlessly off into the wilderness.
Important point: just because the passenger can reach the radio that does not mean they are allowed to touch it. Same with the heater. Leave the fuckin' things alone!

Rule 3 . The job of the people in the back is first and foremost to get drunk and be a nuisance. Demanding irregular but numerous lavatory breaks, pub stops and chips. But they must however have sweets, drinks and gum on hand for the driver at all times - especially jelly babies.

My natural inclination as a drunken, nuisance gob-shite is to jump in the back with a bag of cold beer and I will happily pay over the odds for the driver's petrol if it means I am free of any responsibility. But the guilt can weigh heavy if you don't take your turn and the job of God fell to me for the midweek trip to Birmingham. I tried to be benevolent, I certainly moved in some mysterious ways but ended up being ferocious and Old Testament vengeful.

I put a great deal of consideration into my choice of music. My three passengers all liked The Beautiful South and I could just about stomach their fusion of nice tunes and sarcastic lyrics, so The Beautiful South it was. I happily agreed to pick my passengers up from Rosies and pulled off the motorway early to find a pub as soon as it got to "opening time" (A quaint old fashioned custom).

Winding, pitch black roads led through dark, deserted villages until all sense of direction was lost. The thrill of travelling away to see the Toon when normal people were at work had faded to a memory and the hope of ever seeing civilisation again, never mind the match, seemed increasingly forlorn.

Then.

A light.

A person near the light - would it be too much to hope for?

The light was an opening public house and the person a landlord. All praise to .....er me.

Passengers topped up their lunchtime drunkenness while I scowled into shandy until the landlord introduced us to a group of Blues going to the game and we followed them the 6 short miles to St Andrews where they didn't ambush us and stab us to death - hoorah!

St Andrews was illuminated with naught but a string of 40 watt lightbulbs which meant the game was played on an eerie, gloomy pitch which set the scene for the dark and fantastic fairytale that took place.

Firstly there was David Speedie on loan for the enemy. "We've all shagged your wife Speedie Sp......" began the mass of fans behind the goal until remarkably our old nemesis started shaking his head and waving his arms at us. Then by way of explanation he pointed at the main stand where presumably the long suffering Mrs Speedie was parking her behind.

And in an act of chivalry beyond belief - something I would doubt truly ever happened except for the fact that I was painfully sober - The black & white Army stopped and never sang the song again, even when the little fucker scored one of Birmingham's 2 goals.

That incident alone is worth mentioning but the real excitement was yet to start.

Firstly I got into a heated row with a stranger about the merits of Franz Carr, with me very much on the side of Wor Franzie. Then Franz Carr in a break with tradition (whereby he would wait until I was in full flow in his defence before having an absolute stinker) played the game of his life. Newcastle were excellent and went 1-0 up then were shit at the back. Equaliser. Were brilliant, 2-1, were shit at the back, 2-2. Franz Carr scored, 3-2. Half time.

Tommy Wright was injured - no substitute goalies in them days.

Kevin Brock in goal.

Kevin Brock's first act as keeper? Spectacular, out of character bravery in diving to save at a forward's feet. Where he was rewarded by being violently kicked in the head.

The trainer spent the rest of the match crouching behind the goal and rushing on with smelling salts or cocaine or lighter fluid or whatever it was that suddenly made Kevin Brock the country's finest Number 1. He made tidy saves, he raced off his line to take crosses, he launched swift counter attacks and looked utterly unflappable. Meanwhile Newcastle fought a heroic rearguard action and Franz Carr whizzed off with the ball, taking half the tiring Brum team with him at every available opportunity.

By way of thanks for our earlier politeness Mr Speedie headed his only decent chance of the second half into the arms of our new heroic custodian of the nets. Kevin Keegan and John Hall ran onto the pitch to congratulate the players at the end and Brock, apparently, couldn't remember a thing.

Former NUFC Chairman Stan Seymour died later that night.

It was 6 hours before I was due at work and I was still awake. No big deal except we were still in the pub just outside Birmingham.

We had followed the Blues fans back to Water Orton and the happy landlord (a Villa fan) had happily granted their request for a lock-in.

After a hundred years of staring into my hundredth coke whilst my passengers got ripped to the tits on a hundred cool and delicious pints of beer each, drunk out of glasses that were damp with beautiful condensation......... I cracked and, like a sheepdog manoeuvring a belligerent flock into a pen, barked their reluctant arses into the car.

Halfway back they were all fast asleep and I was in serious danger of joining them. Having let The Beautiful South play through again, my patience with quirky-pop-ballads was strained beyond endurance and I needed drastic action to keep myself awake. Window and foot down. Metallica and N.W.A. cranked up. "C'mon!"

The passengers shifted fitfully, mumbled and eventually went back to sleep as we scorched back up the A1 in a continuous blast of cold air, thrashing guitars and brutal hip-hop. I'm sure they all hated it but in my defence I didn't fall asleep and kill everybody.

In return for their not complaining about sitting in a wind-tunnel or my strident choice of music I dropped everybody off at each of their front doors and went home to bed where street lights still flashed behind my closed eyes, until Kevin Brock made heroic saves from Ice Cube to a "Straight Outta Compton" soundtrack...........

A second later the alarm clock went off.

CHAPTER 19

The Taylor Report

The disaster at Hillsborough is a scar that all footballer supporters carry on their souls. It's something that happened to football fans and while it was Liverpool supporters who took the actual loss we all know, deep down, that it could have been any of us. Football fans' legitimate complaints about how they were being treated had fallen on deaf ears for so long that few bothered complaining anymore.

Two seasons prior to Hillsborough an estimated 13,000 Newcastle fans crammed onto a terrace at White Hart Lane that had a capacity of 8,000. It was hideously cramped and many people's feet barely touched the ground as the crowd moved and the lock of bodies swept you around in a solid tide.

No one panicked because that sort of crush happened regularly at big games and to seasoned gig-goers it was only mildly worse than a festival stage-front crowd. It was, however, desperately hard to breath, you couldn't move your arms away from your sides and if you made the mistake of forcing them up to clap you couldn't get them down again. But people don't die at football matches so we were bruised, battered, uncomfortable and relieved to get out but, apart from the fact we lost to a dodgy penalty and that the fuckers played that ghastly Chas 'n' Dave record at the end, unconcerned. Hillsborough changed that attitude and I don't think anybody who had been at Tottenham didn't think about it when they saw what happened.

On the fifth anniversary of the disaster in Sheffield, Newcastle United played at Anfield and the Geordies brought wreaths and respect for Scousers who appreciated our genuine heartfelt respect for their loss. It was a unique and very moving experience.

It was fences that killed the fans, not the terracing. Some people make that mistake and every time more than a dozen excitable fans spill out onto a pitch there will be some ignorant journalist or some knee-jerk reactionary fuckwit politician (who never had to try and watch a football match through or been squashed up against a bastard steel-mesh) who will demand that the fences are put back up. These people reveal themselves as fools and should be publicly ridiculed or preferably pelted with shit.

In the main, the Taylor Report was a good thing obviously because Hillsborough hasn't been, nor ever should be, repeated. Trouble is the powers that be only really took on what suited them and used the rest to beat supporters about the head with. To the extent that standing up from your seat or dawdling in the aisles is treated at some grounds as dangerous and irresponsible behaviour that is likely to end in somebody's death. It's not.
The fences came down and remarkably fans all over the country didn't immediately rush onto the pitch and start murdering the players, officials and each other.
We can't argue that most stadiums are considerably improved to what we were used to, St James's Park more than most, but football clubs may have been prompted more by the opportunity to make sackfuls of cash than the concern for our safety. Basically, give the same fans the same entertainment but charge them three times the admission by providing a seat.
To this day, however, an important part of the Taylor Report is generally ignored and it's a bloody outrage.
Lord Justice Taylor advised that if large numbers of fans are still outside then the kick off should be delayed. But where's the profit in that - that just causes inconvenience for the clubs, for the police and, heaven forfend, the television cameras.
Saturday November 14th and 7,000 Newcastle fans descended on the capital to see their team play Charlton. There were no Premiership matches that weekend and the game was not all ticket, so outside was absolute pandemonium. Panicking police flapped around giving contradictory information, turnstiles were closed, people were poorly advised by stewards and a few of us ended up paying a wallet-busting twelve pounds for a seat. Fans were still entering the ground with half an hour gone.

Before playing Charlton Newcastle were held to a 0-0 draw in a fascinating televised game with Swindon at SJP where Pavel Srnicek came in for the injured Wright and the television expertise of Lawrence and Tames drooled over the class of Hazard and Hoddle (despite the fact that the latter was rubbish and kept giving the ball away) and all but ignored Martin Ling who was man of the match by a country mile.

So the game at Charlton, against yet another of the teams not so hot on our heels, was as good a time as any to be irresistibly brilliant. Skimming the ball about on a greasy pitch, Newcastle passed Charlton to pieces, defended valiantly and ran out 3-1 winners thanks to goals from the all-action Kelly, the beautiful Peacock as well as a first from Steve "sniffer" Howey.

December 2000, 3rd round replay of the F.A. Cup against Tottenham at St James's Park. Huge crowds still outside due to half the turnstiles being inexplicably closed - fans still entering the ground 25 minutes after kick off.

CHAPTER 20

Europe

The overwhelming majority of football fans are, without question, heterosexual males. Speaking as a member of that majority I can't imagine the extra edge that the game of Association Football could potentially provide for gay men and red-blooded girlies. They have the chance to get something more from the game, an extra fizz, a secret room that we don't get to play in. It is however vitally important to understand that the ability to understand a player's form and fitness and the ability to understand a player's form and lushness are not mutually exclusive. Failure to recognise this fact can lead to severe bruising of the testicles.

Long-serving female fans don't often appreciate the argument being brought up, they struggled enough to be taken seriously over the years without some fool suggesting that they were standing on a rain-lashed open terrace merely to fantasise over the sexual prowess of the likes of George Reilly or Billy Askew so we don't often mention "it". But "it" is still there.

It was the summer of 1988 and the early stages of the European Championships. Wifey (to be) was on the phone talking tactics as the camera panned along the Italians lining up for their opening encounter. Maldini, Vialli, Donadoni are all passed with barely a raised eyebrow then...... Giuseppe Giannini. Long hair, huge brown eyes, dropped phone, excessive swearing, pool of drool. Game starts and our new friend majestically patrols the midfield, moving like a panther with darting glances and an immaculate touch. His passing is exquisite and he apparently plays for Roma.

All of a sudden "our" Italian team is no longer the black and white striped Juventus but Roma.

Before I know it I'm struggling horribly at Italian language evening classes and our first anniversary three years later is spent in Rome.

The Eternal City is captivating, the food scrumptious, the people warm, while sitting on a wall, in the moonlight at midnight with a bottle of cold beer at the Trevi Fountain was blissful.

Our first trip to a European super-stadium rocked us sideways. In the Olympic Stadium just months after the perfect World Cup Final between England and Italy had been ruined by the appearance of the unworthy Germans and Argenfuckin'tina we stood gasping for air at the splendour of our surroundings, too gobsmacked to cry or giggle at the absence of the suspended Giannini.

"Can you imagine seeing Newcastle play here?" one of us said and the other did and we both bit our lips at the very idea.

Pie in the bloody sky isn't enough to describe the leap of imagination needed to get us from grimy cold afternoons in Southend and Barnsley to stages of this magnitude. The friendly and inquisitive locals had never heard of Newcastle United. Their knowledge of the English Second Division was lamentable and they kept asking us if we supported Manchester United.

(The game was a 1-1 draw with Rudi Voller scoring for Roma.)

Fortunately there is more to Europe than wanting to shag Italian footballers. Qualifying for Europe is a magical fantasy for most supporters. Vibrant, floodlit home games and exotic trips into thrillingly different cultures for away games. Not only that but playing in Europe is a big merit badge for your team, partly because it's an exclusive club. When other teams are playing in Europe and yours isn't you feel like a starving urchin with your face pressed against the glass of the cake shop.

In 1992 Newcastle United, staggeringly, got to play in Europe and against Italian opposition as well. We had held the Anglo-Italian Cup for 20 years having won it the last year it was competed for and qualified for this one by seeing off the might of Grimsby Town and Leicester City.

We weren't, however, going to get to go to Roma or even Turin or Milan as the games were against Serie B sides and that meant trips to Lucchese and Bari as well as home games against Ascoli and Cesena.

The competition was mandatory for all Division One sides and our main problem appeared to be how not to win the fucker. All the extra games for little reward seemed crazy but some fans saw it as a once in a lifetime chance to pretend to be a big club. Dave Walker wrote a fine piece about his exhausting train journey to Bari in 'The Mag' and concluded by saying, "This had been a fantastic trip and a memorable experience - one which I will probably never be able to do again."

Some of the exceptionally hardcore and/or rich fans were rewarded for travelling away by getting to share a flight and hotel with the team and directors. And at home? Less than 10,000 for the Ascoli game that was only enlivened by a splendid fight that saw David Kelly sent off and the Cesena game (with both sides already eliminated) that boasted the worst ever Newcastle United crowd. 4,609 fans braved a perishing December night to witness a 2-2 draw with the Italians, wrapped up in gloves, hats and fur mufflers.

As starry-eyed Euro-mantics it wasn't exactly what we had in mind. A time where smiling Mags could meet in the sunshine on the Spanish Steps, share a beer and a pizza in a cafe by the Colosseum and eventually descend on the Olympic Stadium in their thousands never seemed so far away. Who won the Anglo-Italian Cup that year? Anybody?

See?

In 1994 when we spectacularly qualified for the UEFA Cup in our first season back in the top flight, despite losing at Bramall Lane, we danced drunkenly through the streets of Sheffield in celebration and spent the summer dreaming of cold beer in distant taverns.

Our enemies point out that during these last ten years we have won nothing but they know fuck all. Six of those ten years have now seen European qualification and going away in Europe in a prestigious competition is all we dreamed of and more. Fans have travelled in numbers to Spain, France, Holland, Belgium and some other places I would need an atlas to find and it's been fuckin great. Barcelona, despite the pissing rain, was phenomenal and when we actually got to live the dream to see Newcastle run out at the Olympic Stadium in Rome we could have wept with joy if we weren't busy vibrating on the effects of a dozen coffee liqueurs which were far too easily obtainable from the wandering vendors inside the ground. I saw Dave Walker at the game and like the rest of us he was grinning like a fuckin' ninny. Bless him.

CHAPTER 21

The Kevin Keegan Guide
To Getting Rid Of Players

Kevin Keegan's ability as a rabble-rouser is not, and never has been, up for question. The most bitter, long-standing cynical fucker of a fan, people who had endured a thousand broken promises and a lifetime of crushed dreams would be positively bursting with enthusiasm after Keegan had turned it on. He made you personally think you were vital to the club's well-being, with the noise you made and the money you spent on tickets and shirts. Fans thought they really were the twelfth man capable of winning games by sheer noise and force of will which in turn meant the team's excellent performances were partly down to us and that was a constant head-rush and it felt fucking great. And if he had that effect on us, imagine the same thing only one to one on a player. Our lads would be visibly bursting with confidence and opposition teams showing the slightest lack of self-belief would be ripped to fuckin' bits like a wildebeest in a river full of crocodiles.

What is often overlooked however, was that if you crossed him (and didn't apologise really sincerely and really fuckin'quickly) or he could get somebody better to play in your position it was SNAP! bye bye and the door hitting your ass on the way out.
In the November of 92 he transfer-listed 9 players. Kristensen, Roche, Appleby, Garland and Stimson were clearly surplus to requirements but Brock and Ranson had both played important parts in recent games and it seemed really hard on Mick Quinn and Franz Carr. Mick had never been fitter and had come in and scored goals whenever Kelly or Peacock were missing. Franzie's impact at the start of the season had been crucial and his danger as a substitute obvious. Surely both were too important to lose in case we got

injuries. Keegan, as ever, was clearly planning ahead.

It was honest, brutal and with no room for sentiment or regret. The policy never changed throughout his reign and despite the fact that football has a habit of coming back to kick you in the teeth Keegan rarely got caught out and certainly none of the above players returned to haunt us.

Players came and players went with a "thank you very much but sorry, you are not going to be getting a game here anymore - may as well bugger off, eh?"

Years later when Keegan controversially sold Andy Cole to Man Utd it seemed like utter madness but one look at Les Ferdinand in a Newcastle shirt made you think Andy who? Of course most of Cole's fifty or so goals against Newcastle came after Keegan himself had departed.

David Kelly eventually fell victim to Keegan's method of empire building and that seemed desperately harsh. After scoring a hat-trick on the last day of the season in 1993 he never played for Newcastle again. Kelly played like a fan would play - with every ounce of energy given, with passion and with heart. He ran his bastard bollocks off in every game and scored a shit load of goals. Sure, he also missed a shit load of chances but he never hid and he would bounce back to try again like some kind of unstoppable, demon space-hopper. It was impossible not to love the man.

He played for other clubs with varying degrees of success before and after he was here but at Newcastle, where passion and effort are highly regarded, he was a cult figure and that adulation seemed to give him the confidence to be the player he never quite seemed to be anywhere else.

We had three home games in eight days: first we beat Watford 2-0 who got their top scorer (Paul Furlong) injured, had a player sent off for encroaching at a free kick and conceded a really soft penalty after David Kelly cheekily dummied a throw in and the ball hit the defender on the hand.

Midweek we lost 0-1 to Ascoli in a game where Kelly got so enraged at the Italians' gamesmanship (fouling, time wasting and nasty Italian style sneakiness) that he butchered one of their players in a horrible tackle then tried to engage all the Ascoli players and their manager in a fist fight . Marvellous.

On the following Saturday he had already scored two goals against Cambridge when Rob Lee was fouled in the area. Regular penalty taker, Gavin Peacock, picked the ball up to take the resulting penalty but the crowd would have none of it. "Kelly, Kelly, Kelly," we implored. Suitably encouraged, Mr Kelly physically wrestled the ball away from Gav and blasted in his hat-trick. Peacock later scored the fourth in a 4-1 win.

David Kelly finnished the 92/93 season as the club's top scorer and remains possibly the only player in living memory to be applauded onto the pitch at St James's Park wearing a sunderland shirt. Having moved on from Newcastle to Wolves he eventually bottomed out at sunderland and came on as a second half substitute in the 1996/97 derby match . Obviously some fans stubbornly folded their arms or even booed his introduction but a massive percentage gritted their teeth and clapped and Kelly rewarded our remarkable show of affection by missing an open goal.

Whilst at sunderland he still came through to Newcastle to socialise and Mick, a friend of mine who knew Kelly, saw him in the toilets at Julies. "Ya mackem bastard," said Mick with a big smile and Kelly looked him square in the eye and replied, "Do you think I enjoy playing for those cunts?"

CHAPTER 22

7,000 Go Mad In Nottingham

The City of Nottingham's inability to keep one of its teams in the Premiership these last ten years is a source of constant irritation to me. That's not through any affection for either team or any fascination for Robin Hood. It's just the place offers up a tremendous night out. There are myriad interesting bars and there is an unthreatening vibrancy due to the unique lasses to lads ratio which also means that the place is up to its armpits in cute girlies. Everywhere you look there seems to be some dorky-hobgoblin holding hands with a supermodel. Good luck to them. Unlike Leeds where you can smell the testosterone, Nottingham is essentially female. In Rock City, Nottingham also boasts one of the finest live music venues/nightclubs in the country. Damn the football.

British Rail's infrastructure was creaking at the very points under the weight of Newcastle's cavalry charge towards the Premiership. The train stuffed full of happy Mags leaving Newcastle was busy enough but by the time our brothers and sisters from Durham and Darlington had piled on we were all well cramped. The shuttle train from Derby to Nottingham was plain silly. Squashed into each other's faces and singing our daft heads off, the regular non-match going passengers were looking wide-eyed and startled.

When the doors eventually opened in Nottingham we burst gasping all over the platform before scuttling off and squeezing back together again in the nearest hostelries.

The pubs nearer the ground were rammed to the doors and some were refusing new customers - we found one we could get in and began the painful process of getting to the bar where a handful of locals were clinging on for dear life as bouncing, singing loonies swarmed all over them demanding more beer. Outside the weather was grey and freezing but inside the bars it was boiling like a witch's pot and the drinks sloshed down your neck faster than it was possible to buy them.

Notts County, in an unprecedented feat of engineering, had completed three brand new sides to their ground in the close season and we experienced both ups and downs of this new-fangled "all-seater" phenomena. On the upside we got a great view with the steps between the seats being so steep, on the downside we were sat in front of a fat ginger gobshite with a bushy 'tache. On a terrace you could quietly sidle away, here in a crowd of 7,000 seated fans there was simply nowhere to go. So "Tachee" starts shouting abuse at his own team first - "Sheedy you're a fuckin' puff" - before he starts making monkey noises at County's black players and laughing at his own comedy genius. It was only my relative sobriety, wife and rank cowardice that stopped me screaming, "Shut up you fat prick, if there is a master race it certainly hasn't got a beer belly and a ginger moustache so fuck off and die. You twat!"

Fortunately navigating his way to the toilet and back at half-time was beyond the fucker so we didn't see or hear from him again. I didn't hear about anybody falling down the steep steps and breaking their fucking neck but we can always dream.

Sheedy and Peacock scored in the second half to give us a comfortable win from a convincing performance, our only concern being the fan who jumped into Peacock's arms after the second goal which made Gav wince horribly. It would have been a shit way to lose a good player but it must have just been the lad's beer-breath.

We had a friend, Gail, in Nottingham who put us up, fed us then took us out. We were on the bus going back into town that evening and a young local lad complained to his mate "There's fuckin' Geordies everywhere," and he was right. Out of the 7,000 at the match it looked like about a dozen had actually gone home and the pubs were infested with people from Newcastle. Bizarrely we seemed to know most of them and Gail soon got exasperated that we knew more people out than she did. We saw a band (Therapy) at Nottingham Poly then went to Rock City where another band (Sunshot) were playing in the small bar downstairs. They were well shabby but we knew their merchandise seller/lighting guy, a good lad from Stoke whose sister lives in Newcastle. Weirder and weirder, and here like everywhere amongst the hobgoblins and the supermodels were people we knew from the Toon. It was mad, unprecedented and utterly fuckin' brilliant.

After Rock City kicked out we wandered away in search of chips and "cobs" (Nottingham food) with "Toon, Toon, Black and White Army!" echoing round the brightly lit streets. The only cloud on our horizon was the fact that our train the next day was leaving so late but on a lucky streak like this..... we bumped into two lads who were driving back in the morning who had us back in the Toon half an hour before our train was due to leave Nottingham. Encore, Encore.

Notts County have virtually disappeared off the face of the earth. Nottingham Forest, managed by Brian Clough for the last time, were relegated from the Premiership that season despite having Keane, Sheringham and Stuart ("Greatest Living Englishman") Pearce. They only popped up again briefly (hilariously at sunderland's expense) with our games down there being midweek. With their financial difficulties persisting despite Newcastle giving them £5 million for Jermaine Jenas they look fucked to tell the truth and it's a damn shame.

CHAPTER 23

Ding Dong Merrily On High

There has been a growing problem within English football that has never been properly addressed and dealing with it once and for all would make football more enjoyable right across the board. Basically what needs to happen is for the F.A. to set up a highly trained response unit, preferably of ex-S.A.S. servicemen. Suited, booted, armed if necessary -they would be ready to spring into action at a moment's notice, with a licence to operate with extreme and gratuitous force.
This squad of battle-hardened veterans in the peak of physical condition would be paid by the F.A. to sit, in a state of constant vigilance, in front of television sets showing all the major TV channels. Daily newspapers would be delivered to them the second they come off the presses which they will scour thoroughly.

With the unit in place we would be prepared. Then, the second some pompous, over-blown nit of a journalist, football manager, chairman or TV pundit even so much as mentions a mid-winter break in the football season they could explode into action.

Imagine the scene: Terry Venables, George Graham or (fill in name of pundit of choice here) are sitting with Des Lynam and one of them says, "Of course on the continent teams take a break over Christmas whereas here the players have a very hectic and tiring......." Before they could finish the sentence the studio would by overrun by the F.A.'s black clad Unit Of Common Sense who would punch the pundit violently to the floor. They would then be picked up by the neck and have their trousers set on fire. The flames would then be beaten out by the Unit wielding their "Official Football Association Shitty Sticks". Then they would leave.
It would only have to happen once or twice and the whole stupid fuckin' idea

would never be mentioned again and we could all go about our business in relative peace and tranquility. Marvellous.

I don't care if footballers are tired. I don't care if footballers, managers, journalists, TV cameramen and Sven-Goran Eriksson have to go to bed early on Christmas Day and spend Boxing Day working - tough fucking shit.
Who is football for? Who props the game up with their money and who is the entertainment actually provided for? The fans. And fans demand Boxing Day football with no mid-winter break so get the fuck on with it and quit your bellyaching.
To football fans Christmas Day is little except the day before the football. If footballers and managers don't want to work then they can fuck off and become a bin-man - they get Christmas off. Oh, and don't you guys get, like, three months off in the summer with nothing to do but count the vast amounts of money that we, the fans, have stuffed into your pockets?
Here's the deal. We won't complain about how much money you all earn and you don't try and tell us how hard your life is. OK.
And don't give me that new shit about how the money coming in through the turnstiles is only a fraction of clubs' income these days. Who do you think buys the merchandise and who do you think pays for Sky subscriptions? The fans. The same bloody people, so don't try and weasel out of it.
The winters in this country are long, bleak and depressing and the only reason we don't all bugger off and live somewhere pleasant or kill ourselves is because of the football and anyone trying to take that away from us will have to suffer the consequences.

Christmas, traditionally, is a time when families come together. Proper families mind, not the irritating bastards who think they can take advantage of your time and generosity over the festive period just because they share similar blood. Not the people who buy you shitty ceramic nik-naks to clutter up your house that they expect to be able to see on display when they come round to drink all your vodka and eat all your chocolate Hob-Nobs. Not the fuckers who expect gifts, cards and even money - not only for them but also for their revolting fuckin' children that you weren't even consulted about before they brought them kicking and screaming(first) into the world and (second) into your house.

Your proper family, the family you actually chose to be a part of are sitting in the pub on Boxing Day drinking cold beer, wearing their replica strips, shiny new "Toon Army" hats, underpants and jackets and (in some cases) flashing-light, tune-playing Dennis The Menace socks that they got for Christmas, that they think are the funniest thing in the world and that they will spend all day showing to you and to total strangers.

There is a seductive argument that says if we had a mid-winter break then we could have more games when the weather was nice but that doesn't address the problem of what the hell are we supposed to do on Boxing Day without any football. Isn't that rather like a pub not opening on a Saturday night but promising to open up extra early on a Monday morning?

What if the break wasn't over Christmas but the players had January off? Yeah and what if January was mild and February brought a modern ice age? We would be two months behind schedule and the F.A. Cup Final would take place between the opening group games of the World Cup. And the truth is, club chairmen in favour of a break don't want it so the players can recharge their batteries, they want them to play lucrative Far Eastern friendlies so they can try to sell replica shirts to Chinese people.

No, a mid-winter break is a stupid idea put forward by stupid, selfish people who deserve to have their trousers set on fire.

CHAPTER 24

Christmas Presence

The remorseless chill of a Tyneside winter had started to bite and some of our players were starting to look weary. What we needed then and in most years under Keegan was a mid-winter break.

The hundred mile an hour, all-action cavalry charge is a thrilling headrush at the start of a season but Leagues are rarely won by Christmas and then, as in many later years, the team was feeling the strain of an explosive start. Worse still, we weren't taking our chances, Keegan's hunt for a new striker was no secret but his targets and progress were. And while Mickey Quinn was clattering in netfuls of goals on loan at Coventry, Newcastle struggled on with the seemingly inexhaustible Kelly and Peacock, who frankly looked knackered. Kevin Sheedy's contribution from the left was increasingly fitful and Keegan's lack of faith in cult figure Franz Carr was as obvious as it was frustrating.

We slaughtered Barnsley for more than an hour in the freezing cold in front of Tyne Tees Television at Oakwell but lost 1-0. Then at an even colder St James's Park, with the cameras again in (increasingly irritating) attendance we only drew 1-1 with Millwall. Kevin Scott dithered to let Moralee (who we spent half the match booing because we thought he was former Sunderland blonde-poppet John Byrne) score.

Peacock was missing with flu. Beresford pulled a hamstring after twenty minutes which cost us the perpetual motion up the left that had been masking Sheedy's limitations and we had three good penalty claims turned down in the first half.

But on the day our real problem was getting the ball past Kasey Keller . Bedecked in a horrible multi-speckled goalkeeping jersey and sporting a shameful mullet he produced save after save, going to ground time after time on a cruel frozen pitch. He looked unbeatable and we were going to lose. Clearly.

15 minutes from the end and the linesman at the Leazes End chose to punish Keller for his fashion choices and waved his flag for a penalty after a Millwall defender went near Robert Lee in the area. Lee didn't fall or complain, the crowd hadn't appealed, the other Newcastle players looked bemused and understandably the Millwall players were furious. Live on Tyne Tees Lennie Lawrence was apoplectic at the perceived injustice. Kelly blasted in the equaliser from the spot and we went in search of the winner that Keller wouldn't allow.

As if the linesman hadn't been harsh enough, the Good Lord chose to further punish Keller for the misuse of his own hair by afflicting him with premature baldness and the need for spectacles. Although I should point out that this process (somewhat disappointingly) didn't happen before the end of the game but actually took five or six years.

What we desperately needed for Christmas was a goal-scoring machine. We were outplaying all our opponents but our inability to put the ball in the net was letting teams off the hook.

Boxing Day and the pre-match pubs were vibrating with a rumour. Keegan had put a £4 million pound bid in for a striker. No one knew who it was but he was definitely black. God knows why that was relevant or why that was the only information available but that   small snippet of a clue allowed for wild drunken speculation - until someone came up with a name

"It's Les Ferdinand."

The name was muttered along Percy Street, into the town and back again. Strangers were passing on the rumour as solid cold fact to each other at the bars and in the toilets. At the time £4 million seemed an enormous amount of money for one player. Some were excited, some were appalled at the fee and others scoffed, while a few were quietly philosophical. As is always the case in the Toon very few had no opinion and the rumour, along with our admiration of Bront's new light-flashing, tune-playing Dennis the Menace socks, took our minds off our fear of Steve Bull.

Steve Bull's reputation had gone before him as his goals had powered Wolverhampton from the bottom of Division Four into the old Second Division. Two years previous when we first saw him up close we had laughed and jeered as he twice missed hopelessly in front of the Gallowgate End. The derision and the hilarity stopped in the second half when he scored 4 and he had been a constant bloody menace ever since.

Again it was bitterly cold on the Gallowgate terracing and all our new hats, socks, jackets and Toon Army thermal knickers couldn't combat the bitter chill although, as ever, a few drunken maniacs turned up in their shirt sleeves.

Kevin Scott slipped in the box to allow Cook to score for Wolves against the run of play and Newcastle United's long and depressing tradition of ruining their fans' Christmas looked likely to continue until a fine and flowing passing move led to David "Ned" Kelly thrusting the ball into the net with his genitals. (His "doodahs" as he so quaintly put it afterwards). As if to make up for this mildly embarrassing first goal he brutally crashed his second in off the bar from just inside the area.

Scott and Howey did a fine job on Bull but it was Pav who stole the show at the back, outrageously dummying past Bull in the first half and rushing out of his area to charge the ball away with his chest in the second.

Perhaps this year was going to be one of those all too rare seasons where our football team didn't undermine our festive celebrations. Two days later we trooped down to Oxford's appalling Manor Ground and thanks to a long standing jinx and a mad ref got beat 4-2. There were two sizeable crumbs of comfort though: Lee Clark scored his first goal for 24 games which meant the media would have to find something else to wet their pants about and everybody else in the Division were too busy ripping bits off each other to even look like closing our 12 point lead. Teams would go on an unbeaten run then get slaughtered and fall away. Other teams would try and struggle free of the pack but they would be quickly beaten and dragged back in. Tranmere were currently second but Swindon were buzzing again having come from 4-1 down at Birmingham to win 6-4 on the Boxing Day.

CHAPTER 25

No Ordinary Joe

I didn't go to Bristol City away. QPR were due at Middlesbrough and that meant Joe would be coming to Newcastle.

I met Joe Young in the packed corridor of an Inter-City 125 to Newcastle in the mid-eighties. I was working down South, travelling back for the match and he and his mate Keith were QPR fans. Joe was a scruffy bugger, shoulder length curly black hair and tattoos down to his knuckles, while Keith was tall, bony and shifty looking with murderous eyes. My first instinct was to hide in the toilet for the duration of the journey.

Joe came up to speak to me and was actually attracted by the fact that I was wearing a Partisans badge, not with the intention of killing me and stealing my girlfriend as I had initially feared. The Partisans were a little known (and in retrospect, quite rubbish) punk group from Wales who had played at a massive gig with a load of other bands at the Ace in Brixton the previous month. Like me, Joe had been there so we didn't get round to talking about football right away. We chatted all the way to Newcastle then went our separate ways.
A year later we were on the same train going to the same fixture and north of Peterborough before we thought to look for "them lads from last time". Sure enough and with spare seats, there was Joe larger than life but with a different mate and sitting with some Brighton fans on their way to somewhere obscure like Hartlepool or sunderland. They had all been forced by the police to drink their beer on the platform at Kings Cross or throw it away and were sulky and getting sober until we bounced in with two carrier bags full of Stella. Hilarity, cards and more elbow room than we were used to (presumably due to the hearty swearing and beer consumption) made the journey fly over.

Joe, it turned out, was an absolute fuckin' diamond of a lad, hilarious and utterly fearless. He marched into Ossies Bar (the rough as fuck joint on the corner of the Marlborough bus station - now The Dog), ordered his drinks in a painfully obvious London accent, put his money on the pool table and started chatting to whoever was glowering at him the most. We went to Stripes on Blenheim Street and the Waterloo at the bottom of Westgate Road and he did much the same thing. We were terrified for his safety but he never flickered and when we quizzed him about it he claimed to do it everywhere he went. "'Ello, I'm Joe (offering hand), I'm a QPR fan." I never saw anybody not shake his hand.

In Newcastle, where to this day strangers entering so brazenly rarely happens, he had two big advantages. Firstly he clearly loved the place, he had been an away supporter at Keegan's debut as a player and was so impressed by the atmosphere that he kept coming back (he also considered the 5-5 draw between the two sides as being one of the best games ever). Secondly, he was so self-deprecating of himself and his team. When he turned it on he was so likeable as well as being straightforward, honest and downright funny that you had to be a real arsehole to want to hit him.

We swapped phone numbers and met him a few weeks later in London when Newcastle were playing Spurs. Him and his gang of Rangers fans would meet in Moriartys, a bar in Baker Street tube station that served the finest draught Fosters in the world but had no toilet - so you would have to go out the station, past Madame Tussauds and run across the busy traffic to get to the public bogs. We'd meet back there after the game and bearing in mind that this was a time when football supporters where supposed to be slashing each other with razors and kicking each others teeth out, we would end up stopping there for hours talking to fans from Millwall, West Ham, Arsenal, Spurs, Man Utd and whoever else might happen to be in town. Joe, naturally, knew all of them.

When we played at QPR we had a great time in Shepherds Bush and even got into a private QPR Independent Supporters' party thanks to Joe having QPR tattooed on the inside of his lip. The bloke on the door was so stunned that he let about ten of us in on the strength of it.
We had a nightmare getting out of the away section afterwards so in the

following years the Rangers lads insisted on taking us into the home end where despite the fact that we had Newcastle shirts on - everybody was really nice. They took the piss a lot when we lost but it was never nasty.

Over the next ten years we shared more daft experiences in London and Newcastle than my beer-addled memory can recall but it always went on later than was good for us and waking up on a strange floor was always a distinct likelihood. Joe would come and stay with us in Newcastle whenever QPR played in the North East and memorably turned up with four mates, staying for four days at our two bedroomed flat in Benwell. One lad vanished on the Thursday night, never to be seen again after an unfortunate misunderstanding saw us crash out of the Prince Of Wales on the West Road in a flurry of fists and broken glass but the rest of the weekend was excellent. They went dog racing, clubbing and insisted on taking us with them down to Roker to see Rangers beat sunderland 1-0.

Joe was a fascinating mass of contradictions - he cared passionately about football, music (ancient blues, Hendrix , Discharge), politics and his friends but seemed to have a total disregard for his own well-being; he drank way too much, smoked, gambled and mislaid his wallet and house-keys every five minutes. He seemed to pursue only the most doomed and disastrous of courtships with women and could undoubtedly put a strain on any day to day relationship with girls, friends and family with his occasionally erratic behaviour but all these people held him in great affection and I can't remember us ever having a cross word. He could be exhausting and sometimes you felt as though he was a magnet for unnecessary drama but this at least left you with a daft story to tell. He would deliberately aggravate total strangers if he thought they were being twatful which is risky behaviour in a sober environment but in a pub..... Example: we were in the Barley Mow on the Quayside. An American was at the bar boasting to two girls about how he was an actor and had appeared as an extra in Eastenders and Coronation Street. He blabbed on and on in a voice that was clearly loud enough for as many people as possible to hear so Joe says, "Excuse me mate, don't I know you?" Yank bloke smiles. "You're on the telly aren't you? No no, don't tell me, I've got it! You're Foghorn Leghorn!" The place fell about and two minutes later the girls were still there but the American had slipped away.

He would say anything to anyone and once got into the players' bar at Anfield and asked the long haired Darren Peacock to sign his programme "to the lads on the Loft from Conan The Barbarian". Peacock asked if he was taking the piss and Joe started laughing and said, "Of course I'm taking the fucking piss, what do you expect?"

Joe was a care-worker with a genuine concern for his charges but he also traded in rumour and was happy to pass on his wares to anyone who would listen. So and so left Arsenal "because he was a thief", blah blah had to leave such and such club because his colleagues "couldn't deal with the fact that he's a puff". He knew for a fact that a particular manager used to get so pissed that he would regularly sleep in his office and a player, well known to us all, was so notoriously well-endowed that his drunken post-match team-mates would encourage a party trick whereby the player would "play pool with his knob".

"So, Les Ferdinand?" I asked at the Central Station. "What do you reckon?"

It was two years since I'd last seen Joe, he'd lost weight and with his beard I nearly didn't recognise him. I thought it was Jim Morrison.

"He ain't worth £3 million. He hasn't scored away from home for 18 months. Mind you, the bunch of wankers he's playing with haven't helped much."

We talked and laughed, drank and occasionally slept for 36 hours. We went to Brough Park for the dog racing. Joe had been going to unlicenced racing in London to back a mate's dog that was winning all its races and making them a load of money. It only became clear why when the speed his mate had been putting in the dog's pre-match dinner caused it to drop down dead. Joe didn't approve because he was soft on animals and part of his attraction to dog racing was seeing the dogs were loving it as much as the punters.

The two of us went to Boro on the bus which was bizarrely quicker and cheaper than the train and for once we didn't go straight to the pub. Turns out every fan in the country hates going to Boro almost as much as Newcastle fans do and the few hundred QPR fans who went just wanted to get in, see the game and get the fuck out as fast as possible. It was a bit of a culture shock standing with a few hundred pessimistic Londoners away from home compared to the cauldron of passion and blind drunken bravado I was used to with the Toon.

I told Joe and the lads he met in the ground that they would win because Boro were such a God-awful shite football team but they wouldn't believe me. Five minutes in and Boro won a corner. "Come on Boro. come on Boro," shouted the home crowd. At once I began..... "Fuck off Boro! f....", force of habit. I was surrounded by perplexed faces. Unlike when they play us, Boro's fans and team were lacklustre and half arsed but they still managed to kick two of QPR's better players out of the game by half time.

I couldn't get a signal on my radio due to all the shitty pollution in the air so the first I heard of Newcastle's game was the tannoy at half-time. "Bristol City 1 (bated breath all round the ground) Newcastle 2 (groans).

Ha ha, ya fuckers.

Amidst the static and crackling I eventually found our match commentary but the radio bounced across the concrete as Les Ferdinand powered through the Boro defence to clatter the ball into the home side's net and Joe jumped all over me like a fuckin' lunatic.

Newcastle held on thanks to great Pavel Srnicek saves and Bez kicking the ball off the line and QPR held on because Boro were such a God-awful shite football team.

Back in Newcastle we were quietly guzzling lager when a lad came up and said, "I know you. You're Joe, you've got QPR tattooed on your lip." Joe shook his hand and asked how the lad was doing. When he went away I asked who the kid was and Joe said, "Not a fuckin' clue mate but that seems to happen all the time."

Once we got promoted to the Premiership we got to see at Joe at least twice a season again: Moriartys was closed but we hooked up with him and his mates when we could. Paul, a tall shaven headed lad with arms like crashed VW Beatles, Gus, long time piss-taking punker and Ritchie who was polite and quiet despite being sickeningly handsome. We met others but we were always too fucked up to remember everything but the constant laughing. The lads in Newcastle loved them coming up and we were always banging on the door of the White Horse in Shepherds Bush as it opened, wanting to see them.

Les Ferdinand battered us single-handedly one year and we lost 3-0, then we eventually bought Les and went back there the next year to win 3-2. Joe wrote me a letter that we printed in 'The Mag' begging Newcastle fans to call our new striker "Sir Les" and never "Ferdy".

QPR got relegated. For two years in the 90s QPR had been the top placed London team in the Premiership. To Joe's eyes they were being asset stripped and his frustration was obvious but he was equally keen to "find out where the fuck Port Vale actually is" and a new Division meant new adventures. We spoke from time to time but he wasn't going to every game any more and was disheartened by the way his team was heading. Trips abroad were firing his imagination more then anything QPR could serve up.

He would constantly move and lose his damn address book so long gaps weren't unusual over our 15 or 17 year friendship. It was only when his sister rang us up to tell us that he was dead that I realised it had been over 4 years since we'd last spoken.

They found his body in a hotel in Thailand and the official cause of death was respiratory heart failure. Foul play wasn't suspected but the British consulate did point out that 3 or 4 Brits were dying a month out there because of the purity of the drugs.

The daft bastard was only in his mid-thirties, he has a son Matt, his friends and family scattered his ashes on a Brighton beach and I can't bear the idea that I will never see him again.

CHAPTER 26

The Romance Of The Cup

Newcastle United's relationship with the F.A. Cup is a damn messy thing to start looking at but... well.. here goes.......

Basically we've been stalking the bitch for the fat end of 50 years. We had a steamy relationship in the fifties, when we got off together three times and since then we've been following her around like a bloody sick puppy. It's been pathetic, often embarrassing and some fair-minded judge should put a restraining order on us.

Occasionally the old trophy flirts with us - we get to a quarter final, then a semi on, then sometimes even follow her up to her bedroom door for the promise of an actual final and we believe we are truly destined to be together. But she always ends up going off with someone else, the slut. Someone with more money or with some lucky chancer who doesn't love her or understand her like we do.

We've shown ourselves up in public, fighting weedy little teams in her honour, and because we've been so pathetic we've lost, strangers have laughed and the cow didn't even care, she just went off and left us, again, without so much as a backward glance. And we cry and plot our revenge. And we scheme and hope and sit outside with unfulfilled passions boiling inside us until they turn to hate and the F.A. Cup is a worthless whore, we have no interest in her faded charms, she could invite us to the Final again and we wouldn't go and even if we did go we wouldn't care and .... she whispers "see you in the 3rd round next year", we blush then we puff out our chests and say, "You better believe it baby and this time we're gonna' mean business", and, "We'll parade you thought the streets and people will see that we are always meant to be together and that every other team who you went off with was just a dalliance and that we belong together and............"

Pathetic isn't it?

The F.A. Cup isn't romantic. Romance is a shared song or a weekend in Paris or an open topped Cadillac racing across America or murdering a drug dealer together and throwing his body into a river and..... er.... whoops. Ignore that last part.

Whatever.

Romance certainly isn't losing to fucking Wrexham or Exeter or Chester in the bollocking, pissing, fucking rain while some bunch of farmers and sheep-shagging yokels laugh at you.

The F.A Cup is not romantic. "Giantkilling" is not romantic. At best it's a chance for the rest of us to take the piss out of some puffed-up big team who fall flat on their stupid fat arses when they thought all they had to do was turn up in order to beat this silly pub team 10-0. And the rest of us have no actual affiliation with the potential giant killer; you can tell this because as soon as the bigger team scores two goals we all want it to be twenty.

At worst you are the big team and you have to live with the humiliation; in the case of Hereford v NUFC literally for fucking ever! I used to believe that the BBC would get sick of showing Ronnie Fuckin' Radford scoring against us on the bastard Somme but it is clearly not going to fucking happen. And believe me when I tell you I intend to dance on the fucker's grave like it was Margaret Bastard Thatcher's. It's one of the reasons I stay alive.

There is no romance but there is a dream and for years I, like all other Newcastle fans too young to be there in 74, carried an image of my team coming out at Wembley with myself being part of the most amazing support the stadium had ever seen. Just to get that chance, to be actually be there with the world watching... If I saw that - well, you could hang my grinning corpse out for the crows because my ambition as a fan would be complete.

Like so many other dreams pre-Keegan; glory, goals, Europe, we witnessed the reality and the F.A. Cup Final appearance was the only one to prove to be a disappointment. Many of us thought actually being at Wembley to see our team come out would be enough.

It wasn't. Nowhere fucking near. Our fans packing half the ground in a breathtakingly beautiful mass of black and white was awesome to behold and the tremendous noise we made rattled the old wreck of a stadium to its rotten timbers and made our skin prickle and our eyes burn with tears of pride. But seeing that support sent home unhappy because the team didn't match their magnificence is a memory that burns. It's a fire that won't be put out until we actually win the bastard.

Second Division Port Vale came to St James's on January the 2nd 1993 and put up a tidy show, better than most teams we had seen clinging on for a 0-0 that season at least. They had a go. We ended up clobbering them 4-0 with goals from Peacock (2), Lee and Sheedy.
Once again the dream was coming to life. God help us. Next!

CHAPTER 27

Queuing

Queuing. It's our national bloody pastime. Not football or cricket or fishing or golf, queuing, it's what maintained the Empire and won us the war. Apparently. Queuing is the very essence of Englishness - it sets us apart from the savages. If you ignore the queue, push in or march in a different door that has no queue you are morally lower than Hannibal Lecter and are tearing at the very fabric of civilisation. And people will glare at you.

There is no need for queuing in this day and age surely, it's a pain in the arse and everyone hates it. Well, people who have got to queue hate it. People who don't have to queue like nothing better than a good queue, either to take pictures of it for the media or to flounce past it if they are in some way privileged.
The only people who like queuing are old ladies and you can see them gleefully standing outside Post Offices from 8 in the morning even in the most appalling weather conditions. The fact that the Post Office is open all day and that they have absolutely nothing else to do are of no relevance: they like the discomfort because it reminds them of the war. They would be in old lady heaven if somebody reintroduced rationing and sex with American servicemen.

There is an etiquette to queuing and although the rules can be hazy and complicated, transgressing those rules is likely to get you a punch in the mouth. For example: at the supermarket when there are long queues and another till opens up, is it an immediate case of survival of the fittest as to who gets to the new till first? Is shoving or tripping the lame and frail tolerated? Mr & Mrs Carl Cort famously got the rules wrong before the Christmas of 2001 and ended up on the front page of the Evening Chronicle - the stakes are that high.
One of the reasons licensing laws are so stupid is the amount of casualties in

taxi queues resulting from everybody trying to go home at the same time. If some pubs were open all night we could all go home peaceably when we felt like it and not have to get into fist fights with drunken bullies 'cos they nicked our cab. There would be a better spread of fares for the taxi drivers and the rest of us would avoid queuing up yet again at the RVI to get stitches put in our heads. It's not beer or a lack of cabs to blame for this intolerable strain on the NHS, it's queuing and it should be banned.

The tickets for Newcastle's FA Cup 4th round tie at Rotherham went on sale on the morning of 16th of January. I was supposed to be meeting Bront and Kev but got there late.

The queue extended two thirds of the way down the car park so I chose to wait. I was pretty sure Bront and Kev would be further up the queue but more and more people were joining the queue behind me. Wandering up the queue would risk confrontation as well as losing my place. The rewards for pushing in however were obvious - quicker service as well as tickets for the match next to friends - the eternal dilemma.

Satisfied that the queue would move swiftly enough and armed with a Walkman and a paper I chose the chivalrous Englishman's approach of remaining where I was. It was bitterly cold, the wind was brutal and soon blew away my paper. The batteries in my Walkman were flat and the queue was moving agonisingly slowly. Behind me the queue piled up but people were also happily marching past us. I waited, fearing my friends would be too near the front now for me to slip in unnoticed or, worst of all, just served and coming away as I got there. Cursing my indecision I shuffled and glowered at potential queue jumpers. The wind blew so hard we feared the day's encounter with Peterborough would be postponed.

Bront & Kev wandered past and, appalled at my stupidity, told of how people had been meeting friends all the way up the queue and, worse still, some of them had carrier bags full of season tickets and were buying 20 or 30 at a time - which explained why the queue was taking so long. I was 4 people from the front when the tickets ran out and I stamped to the pub twisted with frustration.

The wind got worse but the match was played. Newcastle kept the ball on the floor and mercilessly butchered Peterbough 3-0 with Robert Lee outstanding.

Amazingly there were a growing band of fuckwits very vocally doubting Lee's ability going up to this game. I know it seems hard to believe in hindsight but at least this performance meant they had to move onto someone else.

In 2002 the local news showed eager Middlesbrough fans queuing round the Riverside Stadium for their F.A. Cup semi-final tickets. It was like a documentary about the Dark Ages. Why not go the whole hog and travel to the match in a horse and bastard cart?

NUFC, bless them, long ago introduced a computerised system that supposedly distributes the tickets on the basis of how many games you've been to. Whether or not the system is entirely fair or foolproof is obviously a cause for some concern but it's a vast improvement on deciding who gets to go to the big games by the archaic trial of endurance that is queuing up.

CHAPTER 28

Minnows

Little clubs, man. They're a fucking menace.

Their main purpose for existing appears to be whinging and complaining. We had years of them gnashing their teeth about big clubs waltzing in and taking their best players. Now with most Premiership clubs looking abroad for talent they complain about the big clubs not buying their players.

Play them in a friendly as a favour so they can draw a big crowd and earn a few quid and the jumped-up bloody pub-team cloggers they've stuffed their midfield with will break one of your player's legs. They whine like snivelling little bitches about the money the PFA takes out of any television deals then expect the PFA to pay their players' wages because they've agreed contracts with footballers that they can't afford to pay.

Like an idiot family with a new credit card they spend a load of money they haven't got then resent the "millions of pounds sloshing about in the Premiership". But surely even if they could get their hands on more cash they would, like the idiot family given another credit card, overspend on that as well. Then they expect us to feel sorry for them.

Nobody wants to see clubs going out of business but it's hard to maintain real sympathy with some clubs when you know given the chance they will deliberately try to fuck you off and take your money.

The chance they are given is usually an F.A. Cup tie and the bigger your club is the less likely you want to get involved with these minnows. Not just because of the potential embarrassment of losing but because these minnows often turn out to be voracious piranha fish with an insatiable appetite for your cash and little interest in your wellbeing.

The media may be full of little club "F.A. Cup Fever", the news will be showing jolly old ladies in plastic hats and handknitted scarves (with a thousand bloody badges on) doing the hokey-cokey, showing the world their bloomers, while the ruddy faced local butcher has replicated the club badge in offal, and jumping about in the background are scores of spotty teenagers who have left their

Man Utd and Tottenham shirts in the wardrobe for a week - but the vampiric little fuckers running these clubs are all plotting how to get money off you.

Don't even get me started about those slippery fuckin' weasels at Stevenage who acted like bastards in 1998 then wondered why they got such a hostile reception at St James's. Suffice to say we still wish them nothing but ill and cheer when they lose and will do for some considerable time to come. Thank you very much.

In 93 it was Rotherham with a gun to our heads and, as ever, the minnow/piranha got their pound of flesh when given the chance. They doubled the price of tickets for away fans for the game down there, added 50% to the cost of their match programmes then stood back and let the police get on with abusing us because of a rumour about Geordies with forged tickets.

To this day nobody knows anybody who even heard of anybody with a forged ticket for that game but mounted police were on hand demanding to see the ticket for every Newcastle fan in attendance. Trouble is, being on horseback meant a lot of fans wandered past without looking which lead to a dramatic cavalry charge with fans being clattered by horses and dragged around by the scarf or collar and sworn at for the heinous crime of not noticing that the Nazi on the eight foot horse was wanting to see their proof of admittance.

Meanwhile loyal Rotherham fans were passing on their own £5 tickets to Newcastle fans for £15.

Inside the ground it soon became clear that the club had sold more tickets than they actually had seats for which meant that some people followed a line of seats that ran out before they got to their number. Some of our squad players (Kristensen, Wright, Neilson) were in a large group of fans who had to stand. As is traditional in these circumstances, Newcastle led 1-0, had a good goal disallowed and conceded a scrappy equaliser, while fans waded around in three inches of piss. Well, there's nothing like the romance of the F.A. Cup.

Delighted to have another assault on our wallets approved, Rotherham arrived on Tyneside expecting nothing but our generous hospitality which our board of directors foolishly afforded them when we should have charged their fans fifty quid a seat, given their directors cold tea and one seat between two of them then made their players get changed in the Gallowgate End's stinking fucking toilets.

It's worth remembering at this point that John Hall was so livid about Rotherham jacking up their prices for Newcastle fans that he complained to the F.A. He then bought our allocation and sold them on to us at cut price with our club taking a loss on the deal.

CHAPTER 29

Two Pairs Of Draws

The first Rotherham F.A. Cup game was the second in a series of four draws for Newcastle. It was becoming increasingly apparent that, for the first time since a member of the Royal Family did an honest day's graft, teams were raising their game when playing us. Teams like Manchester United and Liverpool have had a generation or two to get used to this sort of thing but to those of us who had witnessed years of mediocrity it seemed tantamount to cheating. Southend and Luton weren't near the bottom of the League for any other reason than that they were bollocks but when we played them you'd think their very lives were at stake. And their goalkeepers who had spent months conceding soft goals and making twats of themselves were suddenly Gordon fucking Banks.

The Southend game was midweek because the police didn't want two thousand Geordies in town at the same time as the Young Conservatives Conference. A young Stan Collymore playing up front for our hosts was (not for the last time) a bloody pest with his powerful running and quick feet and he was granted the first of two strong penalty claims.

The game should have been over by then. Newcastle dominated the first half; Peacock lashed us 1-0 up and Clarkie chasing a rebounded O'Brien shot was clattered crudely to the ground with the open goal at his mercy. The ref waved play on.

All of Southend's players were 7 feet tall and they tried to pulverise us with a constant bombardment of hoofed balls into our area that Howey and Scott stoutly resisted. Afterwards Southend claimed the upper hand and the moral victory which we all knew was (in Young Conservative speak) "self-deluded poppycock." Newcastle were 15 points clear of their nearest rivals. We could afford to smile, take a breath and drive away.

We played at Rotherham on the Saturday, then were again nicking off work early midweek the following Wednesday to get to a rain-lashed Luton for a 0-0 draw on a pitch made of nothing but mud and sand.

The novelty of appearing live on T.V. had long since worn off by the time Derby County turned up on the last Sunday in January. Games moved, disappointing results and idiotic comments were all we seemed to be getting from Tyne-Tees Television, but this broadcast came with a real sting in the tail.
Witnessing the game first-hand was annoying enough.
Basically Newcastle were doing on a limited budget what Derby had spent a fortune failing to do (i.e. pissing the League). Pre-season favourites, Derby had watched the promotion jamboree disappear over the horizon in a flurry of colour and drama while their expensive forward and defensive lines wondered just who, where and what the hell the midfielders were supposed to be. So they came with an attitude, late tackles, pushing, whinging and time wasting and we had a ref seemingly too daft to see any of it.
 Derby got a dream start with Weasel-boy Gabbiadini crossing for Geordie-boy Tommy Johnson to tap in. Johnson milked it big time then the fun started.
It was an infuriating game - Derby had one other decent chance with Gabbiadini missing an open goal which had us screeching with glee, but otherwise we pummelled the fuckers with no reward until right near the end when O'Brien chested down and blasted in an equaliser to an explosion of joy and relief.
Some of us could barely wait to get home to watch it again because what we had seen was so bizarre and unfair. If we were all cartoon characters we would be rubbing our eyes and doing a comedy double-take. Our view of what we had witnessed couldn't be true. We ran the tape back and, while being mildly amused by T.V. expert Jack Charlton constantly referring to Newcastle as "We", it was all true. We had had 7 (that's seven!) good penalty shouts. Gav had just missed, Kelly had hit the post and Sutton in the Derby goal had made a spectacular save from Rob Lee. It had been massively one-sided and Derby were lucky to get out with the skin still on their arses, never mind a point.
Derby manager (former Newcastle boss, the man who had led us to promotion with Keegan, Waddle and Beardsley- a fondly remembered old friend) Arthur Cox's grumpy old face takes up the screen. And he and I had the following

conversation although unfortunately he never got to hear my part in it:
 Cox:- "We are the better side."
Excuse me?
Cox:- "We had the better chances."
What? When? Bollocks!
Cox -"Newcastle didn't impress me."
You fuckin' mad old bastard. What the fuck were you watching? You are aware that you're not in charge of the team in the stripes any more aren't you? Nurse, bring the bed with the straps on it, oh Arthur have you gone and wet your pants again? We can't let you out in public any more if you're going to show yourself up. Now lie still a minute while we nail the fuckin' lid down!!

Amazingly, despite this display of Arthur shitting where he used to eat and clearly being barmy, Keegan gave him a job when he was England manager and again at Man City.
Whatever, I blame Cox for my sceptical and ageist attitude when Bobby Robson took over at the Toon. I'd seen at first hand that good managers could go off like milk left in direct sunlight and I was frightened. Not for the first or last time I was proved wrong. Thank God.

CHAPTER 30

The 13th Man

If the massed hordes of black and white screaming drunken barbarian maniacs surrounding the pitch are recognised as Newcastle United's twelfth man at St James's Park then the weather sometimes feels like the thirteenth. A midweek February game in Newcastle can't be something any opposing player or supporter looks forward to. It might be wet in Manchester and it always seems to be cold in Leeds but when the wind blows from the North East it's straight from Siberia, we get it first and hardest. And it's brutal.

St James's Park's state of disrepair, which we had long since accepted as normal, with its two open terraces behind the goals and stands to the sides, created a wind tunnel that the icy rain, driving snow and cruel sleet would blast through. Exposed to the elements on the Gallowgate we clung to the terrace with our freezing feet, huddled together against the chill like penguins on an Arctic ice flow.

You don't realise how tough it's made you until you travel south and can wander around in your shirt sleeves while thin-blooded locals cry about the chill. Our players live here so we know they are used to it - opposition players don't live here so they are not and seeing them stamping their little feet and wearing their gloves makes you feel like they are already half beaten.

Before a ball is kicked the enemy player knows that the vicious weather and the passionate and hostile crowd is going to show no mercy in tearing him to shreds. When he knows our team is in form as well.... basically he's in trouble before he gets off the coach.

With our ground essentially being on a hill above the city, walking up there, hardened against the chill by cold beer and enthusiasm, is a spiritual experience. The masses moving out of the darkness towards the light, single-minded in their belief and buzzing with excitement. Even the worst of games can feel magical.

Rotherham visiting shouldn't get the blood pumping even if it's a 4th Round replay but it does if that blood has been mixed with enough alcohol. The first half was awful but we just did enough in the second, with Kelly bundling one in early and Clarkie scoring a peach in the last minute to get us through. Our players flew off to Marbella the next day.

A week later we were given a slight taste of our own medicine, having to travel the length of the sodding country, midweek, only to see our lads go down 2-0 at Portsmouth. We played well enough but Kelly's missed penalty was our best chance. Our lead at the top of the table was down to 7 points.

If walking up to the ground for a match is magical, walking up to queue for Cup tickets is another matter altogether. The Blackburn tickets went on sale on the 11th of February and the whole affair was such a shambles that the club had to change the way it distributed tickets before somebody died. So something good came out of it at least.

Blackburn got away with cutting the amount of tickets they gave us by claiming they had building work in progress. In fact all they had done was rip the roof off their away end.

People started lining up at the iron gates at the bottom of the Gallowgate End at teatime the day before. Three of us had a couple of vodkas in the Newcastle Arms to stiffen ourselves for a long night and, with a half bottle in a side pocket, turned up at 10p.m. At 11p.m. when the pubs kicked out the queue started moving but this was only because people were shuffling up nervously because the first drunken queue jumpers had arrived. The first fights broke out minutes later and the cops were soon all over the place. The queue now stretched past the Strawberry and up alongside the East Stand.

The ticket sellers were cruelly dragged from their warm beds by club officials because the police recognised that the queue was descending into an anarchic mess. The gates were unlocked at 3.30 a.m. and the last remnants of order were lost. There was a frantic stampede up the car park with flasks dropped, sleeping bags scattered and people being trampled underfoot. An old man fell and people looked concerned but didn't dare try to stop as we scratched and stumbled over each other towards the ticket office. Two hours later all 4,800 tickets had been sold.

Now we don't have to queue and we don't have to freeze. A magnificent 52,000 all-seater stadium looks even better as you walk up from the pub but with its roofs and its burger bars beneath we have long since grown soft and thinner of skin. As a result the heating in our house goes on earlier every year and I drive the car to the corner shop.

Not only that, but a visit to Kiev when the wind chill takes the temperature down to minus twenty and 100,000 home fans are demanding your team's blood soon puts our rough, tough, hardened against the cold self-image into sharp perspective. The only consolation as your skin turns to ice is - we're cold, but cockney fans would die.

CHAPTER 31

The Sound Of Silence

Minutes' silences at football are fuckin' great, aren't they?

Oh come on, admit it, they have a raw emotional intensity and a spectacular drama about them that can make the hairs on the back of your neck stand up and your senses positively crackle. Tens of thousands of people stock still, players heads bowed around the centre circle with only the faint click click of a distant turnstile admitting latecomers. Will somebody spoil it? Will there be a shout or a phone ringing or a comedy belch?

Like funerals, they heighten your senses to the point of physical pain. You are so alive it hurts.

What we don't know is who decides on who gets the full one minute respect treatment and who doesn't. The attitude appears to be how much stick the club will get for not observing a minute's silence from the hysterical media. This is because the national media is the keeper of the nation's grief and they tell us how upset we should be. The death of Diana (that woman who used to be married to the queen's son) proved this beyond question.

In the season 2001/02 we were up to our ears in minutes' silences - the two at St James's Park after September 11th were immaculately and beautifully observed to the point that my stifled tears felt like acid in my eyes. That the Queen Mother got a minute's silence for waving at peasants during the Blitz wasn't a surprise but Princess Margaret? Giving her a minute's silence was surely just out of fear of the press. The woman probably didn't know Newcastle United from the bloody Denver Broncos for shitsake. Walter Winterbottom, who managed England dammit, he didn't get a silence? Is the world insane? And surely football and the world should have been brought to a standstill for a minute for Joey Ramone, Kirsty McCall and Spike Milligan.

Seriously, Spike Milligan or Princess Margaret, I ask you?
But the real drama is yet to come, darlings. Many people simply chose to stay in the pub for the silences for minor and former members of the Royal Family. Will we be expected to stand in respectful silence for Thatcher? And if so, how will the former miners in the crowd respond ? Ho ho, that's gotcha thinkin'.

That Bobby Moore deserved and received a minute's silence is without doubt.

Newcastle crashed out the FA Cup to a last minute Roy Wegerle goal, paying the price for not having a go at a Shearerless Blackburn. Keegan wasn't there and for some reason we played defensively. It might have done our busy League campaign a favour but it felt like the end of the world at the time. Our high spirits were crushed and the next week we had to go to West Ham. West Ham had been closing the gap between us with a worrying vigour and losing this match would leave them just one point behind us. Getting into and out of Upton Park was a nervous enough experience with fisticuffs going off all over the place but the 90 minutes was excruciating. The pitch was awful and the pressure immense. Both sides locked horns and ground away at each other. After a messy bad tempered and gruelling game, the teams stepped back and walked away goalless with a point each.

It was the last game Bobby Moore saw. The man who lifted the World Cup for England lost his fight against cancer on the morning of Newcastle's game against Malcolm Allison's Bristol Rovers and the silence that night at St James's was perfect.
Our boys' exhausting war of attrition against West Ham must have taken its toll as they were lacklustre and well off their best in another 0-0 draw. There was an unfair, audible booing as the players trudged off. We hadn't won in the League for 7 games and hadn't scored at all in the last 4.

The following Sunday the media used the minute's silence to stitch us right up. I was selling 'The Mag' at Tranmere instead of standing in a cosy-warm pub drinking scrumptious beer and consequently was stone cold sober, so my testimony is beyond question.
As well as respecting Bobby Moore, the minute's silence was also for

murdered toddler James Bulger and a dead Tranmere official. Somebody behind me, very possibly outside the ground, shouted "Toon Army!" and a stupid little fucker in front of me, pissed on his first shandy, shouted it too. The rest of the noise was people telling him to shut the fuck up - the shushing spread and the Tranmere fans jeered us at the end.

Newcastle's football team sprang back to life in that game and slaughtered Rovers 3-0 with two goals from Lee and one from Kelly. On a pitch that was half rock and half swamp we swaggered back to a form we hadn't seen for weeks and one of our main promotion rivals was blown clear out of the water. We were exaltant. Fans climbed onto the stanchions, flags were brandished, people jumped up and down and saluted our celebrating players. Somebody working for The Daily Mirror must have taken a picture. This picture was reproduced on the back of the next day's paper, a magnificent shot of Kevin Keegan's Black & White Army in full cry. The article underneath described the shame we had brought on our club with our disrespectful behaviour, clearly suggesting that the picture had been taken during the silence. The bastards.
Sometimes to understand how truly despicable the tabloid press is, you have to be at the sharp end of their spite. It tastes nasty and it's unfair but it puts them into sharp unforgettable perspective and the next time they start pretending to be "the fans' champion" you can spit in their eye, laugh or turn away.

CHAPTER 32

Splashing The Cash

As things stood at the start of the 2002/03 season, Newcastle United had spent £125 million on players in ten years. That's one hundred and twenty five million pounds. On players.

They have also spent over £100 million on redeveloping St James's Park.

If anybody had told us that was going to happen in 1992 we wouldn't even have argued. We would have been much too busy phoning the nearest lunatic asylum after we'd climbed out the window and sprinted up the street. What's the point entering into a conversation with somebody who is certifiable, probably dangerous and gibbering loads of nonsense. But here we are.

It really is staggering, in fact it's a total headfuck if you think about it for too long, so let's change subject.

Newcastle United, with perennial crowd-scapegoat Mark Stimson making a rare appearance in the team, battered the living bollocks off Brentford at St James's Park in a scintillating display of fantastic free-flowing football. The score was 5-1.

Six goals in total (call me Dr Maths).

Ask anybody who went to that game to describe one of the six goals and they can't. This is because the one event from this game that stood out was so monumental that it obliterated all other memories of it. Most of you know what I'm going to say, it was such a big deal.

Robert Lee scored a goal so outrageously good that it made David Beckham's much-seen strike from the halfway line against Wimbledon look like a rudimentary tap-in.

A ball was knocked over the Brentford defence and Benstead in their goal rushed out of his area to boot clear. From ten yards inside his own half Rob Lee chested the ball down and whacked it straight back over the desperate

Benstead and into the Brentford net.

Goal Of Forever. We had never seen anything like it and went instantly bananas. The ref had apparently whistled for an offside in our favour and the goal didn't stand. Our disgust was such that we booed the ref off even after winning 5-1 and Rob Lee looked utterly gutted.

Kelly, Bracewell, Clark (2) and Lee (from a perfect Stimson cross, by the way) scored for us with Scott coolly knocking in his own net for them. It was the 6th of March and it was our first Saturday home game since the 16th of January which, coincidently, was also the last time we had won at home in the League. We didn't and still don't like not playing on a Saturday. There's no logical reason for it but there is no reason why the team always underperforms in white socks, white shorts or with three centre-halves - it's just how things are. With Peacock, Sheedy and Killer all injured plus Steve Watson and Alan Thompson away representing England in Australia in the World Youth Cup we were down to the bare bones so finally, after months of speculating over which striker Keegan was going to buy, he bought a right back and a left winger. Scott Sellars cost £700,000 from Leeds and Mark Robinson £450,000 from Bradford.

Who? How much? Was the transfer market going mad?

We got our first look at the new lads in a midweek game against Charlton. Robinson looked solid but Sellars looked short of a hearty breakfast or two and clearly was averse to meat pies and Guinness. Scrawny little bugger.

Rob Lee scored early, charging through the centre of the Charlton defence about half a second after the kick off. Another 5 goals were surely on the cards except our defence bolloxed up and it was soon 1-1. Sellars put the most exquisite free kick right on Kelly's head so it was 2-1 at half-time.

Charlton's second equaliser came from the sort of defending that has earned Newcastle United such a dodgy reputation over the years. It came from a corner. A corner that we took. Then, as happens to us once in a while, everything went daft. Passing the ball back and badly, defenders bumping into each other, slapstick falls and multiple brain seizures until Charlton scored.

The game finished 2-2 and as usual it was Stimson's fault. The fact that he wasn't on the pitch was of little relevance. Everything was always Stimson's fault.

Friday the 12th of March and Newcastle United paid £1.75 million for Bristol City's top striker, Mr Andrew Cole.

CHAPTER 33

The Role Of Live Music In The Life Of The Modern Football Supporter - Discuss

When Egil Olsen was manager of Wimbledon he once famously said, "I don't like any music. I prefer silence" it seemed like the weirdest thing in the whole wide world. Surely everybody's life should generate some sort of ongoing soundtrack. The music you listen to says more about you than what your job is or what you wear. Potty Old Egil's statement could as easily have been, "I don't like clothes - I prefer to walk round the streets nude, with my bollocks on display for everyone to see" as far as I understand it.

Ian, a friend of mine, claims that most young adults reach an age where they decide between music and football as to what is their true obsession and that only a few of us choose to walk both paths. True, very little music can match the thrilling headrush of a ball ripping into the back of the net in your team's favour but you can't underestimate the value of paying for a ticket for something that isn't remotely likely to have you drowning in a black lake of alcohol-fuelled depression like the Toon losing can. (Unless you accidentally go to see Celine Dion but that would serve you right.)

But I don't see it as being a choice between one or the other - well at least it shouldn't be. A group of us rushing out of the match and sprinting across the Haymarket and still missing half The Stranglers' set at The City Hall was a rare need to compromise.

Going to see bands and realising that life can actually be fun certainly saw some of us through the last days of mad Ruud Gullit's reign and going to see bands when the Toon are rocking just feels an extension of your general euphoria. Whatever music you like it sounds even better belting out loud before you go to the match or when you've come back from a rollicking good win.

If, like Egil, you couldn't give a damn about music do yourself a favour and skip the rest of this chapter. We lose 2-1 at Swindon and the editor of 'The

Mag' gets hit on the head with a duck.

I was working for Paint It Red - a North East listings and entertainment magazine back in 92/93 as music editor. For a regional rag we had massive bollocks and got exclusive interviews with, seemingly, anybody we wanted. The place was constantly buzzing with good photographers, great designers and cocksure writers rattling off small works of genius despite the telephone ringing all fuckin' day. The office was above The Riverside, a fantastically shabby live venue that thousands would squeeze into until the walls dripped with condensation. Nirvana played their first UK show there, The Happy Mondays played to about fifty people in their early days as, later, did Oasis (Liam resplendent in pink shell-suit - they played three times in total and only got attacked once). The Riverside was staffed by great people (who knew to put a band on at a late hour if the Toon were playing) and their offices were opposite ours and folk buzzed between the two all day. It was generally madness; things like trying to make a phone call while The Beastie Boys were shouting and jumping about the place only seem extraordinary years later.

Friday the 12th of March, the day before Newcastle played at Swindon, and I was on the phone trying to explain to the nice girl at A&M Records why somebody from a North East magazine would want a guest listing for a sold-out show in Bristol when Gordon came in grinning.
"What do you think of the new signing?" he beamed.
"Yes it's for me, what... sorry, hang on," (hand over phone), "Sellars or Robinson?"
"Nah man, Cole."
"Who? What? Yes I'll be reviewing it," the world was spinning way too fast and, "Gordon wait there, you fucker! What are you grinning at? Don't move!" Eventually I hung up. "Explain everything slowly, what are you talking about?"
Andy Cole had signed for £1.75 million and was in the squad for the next day's game. I didn't believe him and frantically jabbed at the buttons on the car radio while I raced over to Mark's house. He hadn't heard the news either.
The two of us giggled and stamped our happy feet every half hour, on the half hour, as Radio 5 repeated the news as we made the traditionally erratic journey down the A1.
Round the enormous Aston Expressway and thus Birmingham, we plummeted

south into Bristol. Frazzled but still jibbering with excitement we missed the first band (Gallon Drunk) with the time it took to get served in the Union Bar Mark, bless him, was always up for anything different and as open minded as you like but the second band, Silverfish, traumatised him forever. Fronted by a shaven-headed Glaswegian woman screaming over tuneless thrashing guitars and hammering drums - he seemed genuinely appalled. The aggression and energy were fantastic to me but Mark looked as if he might actually cry so we went back to the bar. To this day I can't recommend a band to him without getting a wry suspicious look and a mumbled complaint about Scots women pushing dustbins down the stairs.

After Therapy had done their usual 45 minutes of industro-punk mayhem we raced down to Devizes to stop with my step-brother and the next day went to Swindon. Mark was further mentally scarred at the match by getting hit square on the back of the head by an ornamental plastic mallard. Someone shouted, "Duck", and threw it. The aquatic projectile was being pelted around the away end with people shouting, "Duck", and then laughing hysterically.

We lost 2-1 because ref Graham Poll missed a blatant handball that led to a Swindon goal. Andy Cole came on as a sub after an hour and barely got a kick Our traditional friendly banter with the Swindon fans ("You're Scotch and you know you are" met with "You're Welsh and you know you are". and then singing. "We hate sunderland more than you do") was getting spoiled by a bad tempered game but the score of Notts County 1, West Ham 0 brought mutual cheers and had us applauding each other at the end. How lovely.

We spent the Saturday night wandering round half empty, silent pubs where the locals stared at us like we'd just fallen off the fucking moon.

A few days later: big match atmosphere, a mass of bodies, heaving back and forth and from side to side. Eager with a buzzing anticipation. Fists pumping in salute - "TOON ARMY Toon Army TOON ARMY Toon Army". The arrival of the men in black and white shirts brings an ear-rending roar of approval. Stiff Little Fingers live at The Mayfair Ballroom fronted by adopted Geordie Mr Jake Burns. The band explode into "Fly The Flag" and the crowd are instantly a frenzied thrashing mass, bursting with the heady mix of too much beer, rock and roll football and old-school punk rock. They sing all the words and the guitar breaks I interviewed a lad from a band in sunderland (the mighty Leatherface) who said he walked out of the gig in disgust. How cool is that?

The Riverside and The Mayfair no longer exist. For all our city's massive improvements these last ten years, we are poorer for their passing.

CHAPTER 34

Ain't No Feeble Bastard

Kids today, they think they invented fighting rascism.

One thing that really gets on my tits is the idea that being vocally anti-racist means that you're some sort of Politically Correct liberal lentil muncher with a guilty conscience. A cardigan wearing, vegetarian, whiny ninny who attends protests, wears the T-shirts and the badges, writes indignant letters to magazines and who thinks that the world could be all fluffy and lovely if only we would all be nice to each other for a change.

The other thing that really fucks me off is the idea that the people of Newcastle were all ignorant evil bigots until about 10 years ago.

In the 1930s, Oswald Mosley who, as you probably know, fancied himself as being the English Hitler. What a lot of people don't know is that twice he came to Tyneside with the intention of stirring up hatred. Mosley and his dimwitted gang of knuckleheaded thugs were paid to come to intimidate and bully our uppity unions.

Both times him and his hired goons got the living shit kicked out of them and had to scurry back down south with their tails between their legs. After a first failed attempt in Gateshead he came back and the local papers described three days of running battles on the Town Moor. There was no mention of how many badges or T-shirts were sold.

My grandfather lived in Newcastle and, God bless his cantankerous old soul, fought fascism. Not by waving a banner and buying the new Billy Bragg album but with a great big fucking tank. It worked too.

Newcastle United, like a hell of a lot of other teams and the country in general, had a nasty, ugly and embarrassing problem with racism in the late

70s and early 80s.

On the other hand Muhammad Ali, the greatest ever sportsman, as well as being an uppity black guy with a big mouth, opened Eldon Square in 1976 and the massive crowds bloody well loved him.

Apologists claimed that abusing a player because of the colour of his skin was no worse than picking on a player for being fat, ginger or bald but eventually it became apparent to the vast majority that making monkey noises at somebody (who isn't Peter Reid) just makes YOU look like a twat.

By the mid-80s racist chanting was only from a minority of dickless, inbred fuckwits and while the National Front would turn up and try to sell papers outside the Gallowgate end they got considerably more hassle than sales. People would abuse, spit at, threaten and belittle them to such an extent that they must have found something else to do with their time - because they stopped coming.

A succession of black players turning out for the club helped: Howard Gayle and Tony Cunningham both had their own songs ("He's black, he's broon he's playing for the Toon..."), Mirandinha was worshipped and Franzie Carr adored but Andy Cole blew the shrivelled pathetic little balls off the remaining dismal fuckin' bigots because he was black, confident and, unlike those who came before him, utterly brilliant.

Even the stupidest, most sloped-browed, hate-filled, repressed homosexual (waaaay too much shirts off, male bonding denial you guys - come out of the closet, accept who you are), jumped up, badly tattooed, BASTARD could see that, if there is a master race, then compared to Andy Cole, IT ISN'T FUCKIN' WELL THEM!!

There are so many black lads in the Newcastle squad these days that the vast majority of fans don't notice or care what colour a player is. And a lot of good work by a lot of good people means that the bigots who haven't been swept away know to keep their pathetic opinions to themselves - but constant vigilance is required because these insidious cockroaches will always try to crawl back and they must be stamped out. By any means necessary.

20th of March 1993: At SJP the atmosphere was rejuvenated. Everybody seemed eager for Cole to do well, so he could fit in quickly and feel welcome.

He was given a warm reception and masses of applause and encouragement at every touch. The players extended this still further, seeming more interested in teeing up Cole than scoring themselves. 1-0 up at half-time courtesy of a deflected Rob Lee shot, Newcastle came out for the second half and ripped County to shreds. Cole missed a couple of half chances to mass disappointment before Kelly swept us 2-0 up, who then powered in the third with his head after an exhilarating move involving Cole and Lee put Clark clear down the right. Clarkie put in a great cross and Kelly's finish was emphatic. Newcastle were pissing the game but an air of disappointment still hung over the game until Cole got the ball with his back to goal at a difficult angle. He swivelled and lashed a shot so ferociously that the keeper didn't blink, never mind move, and the crowd went ballistic.

The pubs post-match were vibrating - Cole was class and had exactly what we'd been missing - lethal bastard finishing. Now who wants some? C'Mon!

In the "The Definitive Geordie Dictionary" there will be a picture of my mate Jane next to the definition of "Canny-lass". She was well served, leaning on her fella and grinning like the beer was free. "Coley man...he's bloody marvellous and just wait 'til he gets a had-o-them bloody mackems. Ha haa!" Bless her.

CHAPTER 35

Keegan and Me

I hated him. We all did.

When Liverpool slapped us silly in the 74 F.A. Cup Final Keegan was to blame undoubtedly. Malcolm MacDonald had virtually promised us that we were going to win and Keegan made our best player look silly. In fact, he made most of our players look silly on the day, the swine.

And then Kevin Keegan the player went on to become the most popular sportsman in England and, like virtually everybody else of a certain age, he was my hero and no amount of shoddy adverts peddling anything from Brut to Bullworkers was about to change that.

The clever thing was playing for Hamburg. The experts were all busy pointing out how much he had improved since he went to Germany but that was largely irrelevant. The important thing to us tribal types was that first and foremost England's best player could never be the enemy. Playing in a different country he couldn't score against your team, dive in your penalty area or celebrate at your expense. The only time he performed in this country was heroically for the national side or bravely carrying on after falling off his bike in Superstars. So you could love him unconditionally. I know I used to turn up early to grab the number 7 shirt in my short and unspectacular pub-team career.

Attempting to play like Keegan meant enthusiasm, effort and bloody mindedness, overcoming some of God's more awkwardly placed stumbling blocks. Slow, one footed, and feeble with a conscientious objection to heading the ball I may have been but the fat, lazy and the blind octogenarians who made up the rest of the Kings Arms' C Team knew I would run about for 90 minutes and never stop trying. Fruitlessly mostly but thanks to Kev I had principles.

I was physically giddy with disbelief and excitement when he signed for Newcastle. It was hard enough getting my head round Keegan in a black and white shirt at the time but with hindsight Keegan coming as a player was the most important single event at the club in nearly fifty years. Everything we live with now from magnificent stadium to a squad chock-full of internationals can be traced back to Keegan signing as a player. It was the birth of a mutual understanding that led to him returning as a manager and starting what others have improved on.

In the first England squad announced after he joined Newcastle, Keegan was omitted. He got cross at the lack of a call from Bobby Robson and retired from international football. Convinced of the anti-Newcastle bias at the F.A., most of us sided with Keegan and against Robson. A point, that in retrospect seems daft and embarrassing.

Keegan played two years, scored goals, got us promoted and flew off in a helicopter.

For years fans would shout, "Keegan Keegan Keegan" whenever a police chopper flew over a ground we were in.

I have to be honest, I was appalled when he replaced Ossie Ardiles as manager but I rejoice in being spectacularly wrong about stuff.

His infectious enthusiasm is recognised and well documented but his absolute refusal to put up with the third-rate shit that his predecessors endured was vital. Appalling training facilities were improved, money promised by the board would be delivered and standards throughout the club were raised. His enemies in the press point at early hissy fits and walkouts but he got what he wanted and what he wanted was what was best for the club.

He put voltage into Newcastle fans' natural swagger and made us believe we could expect and demand more. His detractors claim he leaves no job finished but pick any team at the bottom of the country's Second Division in any given March and offer them survival that year, promotion as Champions the next, Europe the next and being the best side in the country two years after that and not many will tell you to "fuck off".

1996 - Best side in the country? That year, undoubtedly. No one who saw the game that we lost 0-1 up here to Man Utd could look you in the eye and tell

you we deserved to lose that game. If we had even drawn we would have won the League. The cruel results at Blackburn and Liverpool are red herrings. Steve Bruce says the game his team won here gave them the belief to continue an incredible unbeaten run. Without that one result they wouldn't have done it. Basically the 5-0 result we enjoyed the next season came a year too late.
Like all of us, Keegan was mentally flattened by the injustice of that season but, unlike us, he can and did walk away.

It is dangerous to worship people because all are flawed and KK himself wasn't perfect.
In a fit of temper he scrapped the reserve side and he ignored youth development. Good local players saw there was no room for them at Newcastle under Keegan and went elsewhere - Michael Carrick openly admits as much. His loyalty to some players regardless of form or fitness was admirable but sometimes destructive. In 92 he had a bewildering loyalty to Sheedy; Keegan kept playing Mike Hooper even though his confidence was obliterated; Rob Lee would be looking shattered and Beardsley way off his game but they were never in any danger of being dropped.
He seemed to regard a tactical substitution as something other managers did. Possibly he saw them as an admission of not having picked the right team in the first place but to this day I lie awake at night thinking about that Man Utd game, wondering why the hell he didn't bring Clarkie and Gillespie into a tired team that had no more to give for the last 15 minutes. You could see them straining at the leash on the bench while the players on the pitch were shot.
His tactical and coaching abilities were put under the microscope as England manager and, by his own admission, he was found wanting. But if Graham Taylor had possessed a similar self-awareness then Bobby Robsons's legacy as England manager wouldn't have been so depressingly wasted.

But the thing that bugs me most about Keegan isn't his fault. It's the Newcastle fans who won't let go. They seem to have this twisted belief that under Keegan we beat Man Utd 5-0 every home game and only played in seven goal thrillers away.
We didn't and he's not our manager anymore. Get over it. Let it go. Surely the most important thing Keegan taught us was that you can't live in the past.

He's the manager of another team now, he's the enemy. Manchester City's progress would be to our detriment so it is imperative that he fails.

Having said that, I still adore him. He had vision and belief beyond our wildest dreams and he made us all feel part of something special. He was, and is still, the best rabble-rouser on the planet, capable of generating a tidal wave of enthusiasm and ambition that sweeps all before it.

Unlike Dalglish and Gullit who tried to change us, Keegan gave us what we wanted. Beautiful, reckless, attacking football. Dalglish saw an early goal as the first step towards three points whereas we and Keegan see an early goal as the first of 5. Gullit, mad as a coconut by the end, presumably saw an early goal as proof that he was right and everybody else was wrong. And that the moon is a flying omelette.

Keegan put us where we are by raising the club's profile - he gave us Rob Lee, Peter Beardsley, Andy Cole, Les Ferdinand, Ginola, Asprilla, Batty, Albert, Fox, and who else on the planet could have convinced Alan Shearer to sign for Newcastle United instead of Manchester United?

Finally, the thing I like about Kevin Keegan, the absolute best, is the thing the media see as a weakness. The "Luv it" speech on Sky after the Leeds game is held up as a prime example of him "cracking and losing it". Him being "too emotional".

Bollocks!

It was absolutely fucking brilliant. His passion, fuelled by injustice, spilling into a righteous rage was Keegan at his shining best and at that moment in time it was the finest thing ever.

The press attacked Keegan in 93 over an outburst that is generally forgotten. Newcastle had lost 1-0 at Watford and a fan within earshot accused the team of not trying. Keegan jumped down his throat, the media wailed about people being entitled to their own opinion and Keegan's verbal assault as being unseemly but to those of us sick of the minority of our own fans whining in the face of our best team in years, it was exactly what was needed.

Getting in there and saying what you think. Heart on sleeve and bollocks to those who don't like it.

CHAPTER 36

Who Wants To Be The Ref?

Who went to school with anybody who grew up to be a referee?
Nobody. That's because they are not indigenous to this planet. They are shipped
in by the F.A. on a Space Shuttle from the planet Gormless where there is no
common sense, where a sense of humour is punishable by death and the last
sense of perspective died of loneliness at the turn of the century. When they
turn up here, all pale and emaciated, they are given a book of rules to learn
but they are never, ever allowed to see a football match before they take
charge of one.
They firmly believe, with the last fibre of their being, that 50,000 will turn up
and happily pay money to see them do their job. They are convinced that
football is not a form of entertainment and that nobody actually likes it
because what we all really want to do is watch a really fussy little twit take
revenge on the world for his own sad inadequacies - and they are legion.

To this day some referees don't understand the difference between a player
celebrating a goal in front of his own fans and a player taunting the
opposition's fans. You still see them disrupting celebrations, blowing their silly
little whistles and even booking players for "over-celebrating". If a player
scores a goal and then waves his cock (his penis OR his pet rooster) at the
other team's fans then, maybe, he should be booked. But if a player scores and
celebrates in front of his own fans he is entitled to walk along the crossbar
juggling the half-time oranges, build a human pyramid with his team mates
and impregnate his girlfriend while we cheer him on. OK?
OK.
Already in the 92/93 season we had seen Lee Clark firmly chastised and
threatened by the official for celebrating a goal by snatching a bobble hat off
a youth's head, pulling it over his eyes and feigning comedy blindness. Years

later we lost Tino Asprilla from a vital Champions League game because he got booked for putting his shirt on the corner flag and waving it above his head like a flag. This is the entertainment business darlings and the punters love it, so back the fuck off.

Birmingham had reacted to the threat of relegation by buying fifty new players every week for a month, one of whom was Andy Saville from Hartlepool who celebrated being back in the North East by trying to start a fight with Steve Howey in the first minute. This got the crowd on his back so he celebrated by scoring and setting up the goals that put Brum 2-0 up at SJP (in front of the bloody live cameras) by raising his clenched fists at the Gallowgate End. This the ref ignored

After an hour of passing our guests to death Pav banged a long ball up top which Sellars controlled and crossed for Cole to score. The other players leapt all over him but the ref was over like a shot, pulling players apart and sending them back to their own half. What could he have been thinking? Our players were celebrating a goal in front of their own fans and we were still losing so we were hardly likely to be deliberately wasting time. Perhaps he just wanted to be on our end of season video.

Sellars crossed for Lee to equalise but the winner wouldn't come, although since West Ham had drawn 0-0 with Millwall in a lunchtime kick off we could just about live with it.

However mad the ref and however bizarre the game, nobody was paying Newcastle United the slightest interest the following weekend. All season long 'The Mag' had been full of fans complaining about Newcastle's achievements being ignored by the national media but as we battered Cambridge 3-0 at the shabby Abbey Stadium the game may as well have been played on the ref's home planet.

"You're fuckin' jokin'?"

Mark R, the lad who had whizzed us back from Nottingham in a sensible four door Astra had bought a new car. A gusset-moistening Honda Prelude designed specifically to put off potential gooseberries by having a mere three inches of leg room for the rear seats. I was already sitting with my feet at quarter to three and head in my lap when we got to Mark J's house. My own considerable discomfort was forgotten as Mark, taller and wider than me, complained at being forced in next to me.

"Ow, ow, this is stupid - get a proper fuckin' car."

By the time we stopped for petrol halfway down the A1 we were both numb from the waist down and had to crawl across the forecourt until any feeling or use returned to our legs.

It was F.A. Cup semi-final weekend with both games being played at Wembley. Sheffield Wednesday (with Chris Waddle) saw off Sheffield United (with Alan Cork's Gandalf-lengthed beard) and then Arsenal overcame Spurs to set up what turned out to be the most awful and tedious Final the competition had ever witnessed. It finished in a draw and Wembley wasn't even full for the equally mind-numbing replay. If this was the sort of team Newcastle had to beat in order to win stuff then we were going to be up to our damn ears in trophies by the turn of the Millennium. No problem.

Newcastle cruised through the game 3-0. Howey nodded one in while Kelly and Cole both scored after balls were knocked over the top. Then, with a game due midweek, we conserved our energy by passing it about and keeping possession while stupid fans complained. Afterwards, eager to hear glowing reports of our game, all we got was two hours of people complaining about The Grand National. It was the year of two false starts, the second of which some jockeys ignored and kept going while others waited for a restart which resulted in a horse called Knob Cheese winning at about 8,000 to 1. Something like that. Who cares?

CHAPTER 37

Where Were We When We Were Shit?

"Where were you when you were shit?" sang the Liverpool fans at us during the 2001/02 season. One kid behind me said, "We were all here last week. You should have seen us man, we were bloody awful."

Well, the facts are that Newcastle have always stuffed their own ground out and taken up our full allocation for Anfield when playing the Scousers - if you don't know that then where were you, eh? But it is a question we get asked a lot, by jealous or stupid rival supporters, so I have some answers: they might not be the right answers but that's not going to stop me inflicting them on you.

Firstly, the low attendances that our enemies like to wave in our faces are deceptive. There were times pre-Keegan when we were jammed solid into St James's Park with no noticeable gaps in the home terracing. The attendance would be announced as 26,000.
The capacity was supposed to be 36,000. Where the hell another 10,000 people would wedge in God only knows. But it gets interesting because in the promotion season, post-Hillsborough, the SJP crowd was limited to 30,000 and we somehow had loads of elbow room. The first 3 or 4 steps in the Gallowgate End had nobody on them which suggests that, for one reason or another, pre-Keegan, the counting wasn't up to scratch. Somebody did once tell me that the club paid rates to the council on a sliding scale, depending on attendances and that announcing lower attendances meant the club saved money. But as this would surely have been illegal it couldn't possibly have been true.
Even if we were getting bigger crowds than were being announced we weren't getting 52,000 so where have they all come from? Glory hunters?
Hardly. It's been ten years - a good proportion of the present crowd would have been in nappies or not even born when we were last seriously shit and

what you've got to remember is that we were quite shit for a hell of a long time. Manchester United fans like to boast that they were getting massive crowds even after they were relegated but they bounced straight back with a thrilling young team. Newcastle United were in depressing decline for years. We lost Waddle, Beardsley, Gascoigne and a lot of demoralised fans.

But calling the returning fans "Glory Hunters" misses the point. Newcastle is a unique and exceptional city where virtually everybody is a Newcastle fan. Even if they don't go to the game every week 99% are there in spirit and they have got a pretty good idea of what's going on.

I've got a mate, Shaun, who hasn't been to a game for 5 years. Does he care less or is he less passionate about Newcastle United than me? Naturally I tell him he is - but he's not. (Mind, if he got tickets for a Cup Final and I didn't I would break his arms.)

The whole city breathes football inside and outside the stadium, the glory and the pain envelops the entire populace. Can you honestly believe that there are 20,000 fans in St James's Park who used to support somebody else, who changed teams because Newcastle suddenly got good? Or were they always Newcastle fans who just turn up more often now and in some cases bring their kids?

Obviously in some cases it would have been better if some of the whingy-faced bastards hadn't bothered and some of the people who just sit and grumble instead of supporting their team should have their bony white knuckles prised off their season tickets in favour of young, drunk, excitable, teenage, shouty types but that is a different point altogether.

Where was I? Standing on the Gallowgate, feeling right at home. I was still there when we got good as well, composing bad tempered, misspelled rants for 'The Mag' about being forced to sit down at the football. I had been in the seats 3 times in my life and I didn't like it. No atmosphere, no jumping around the terracing when we scored, no heaving, breathing mass of pure tribal black and white energy.

The new stand taking shape behind The Leazes End was impressive but at the same time it cast a shadow over my soul as Newcastle came out to face Barnsley on the 7th of April, with only 3 more home games before we were to be forced off our beloved terrace forever and into the clean, safe and anodyne world of sitting. Sitting nicely with our hands folded on our laps, clapping politely and sipping our tea. Urgh.

Newcastle butchered Barnsley like infected livestock, burning the carcass of their self-respect on the fires of our glory. It was 6-0 and it could have been fifty. Cole rattled in his first hat-trick (left foot, right foot, header) before sliding on his knees in front of an ecstatic Leazes end. Clark and Sellars both scored and a gleeful Johnny, Johnny, Johnny, Johnny Beresford finally scored his first goal from the penalty spot.

The walls of the Newcastle Arms were rattling with the celebratory din. I took a moment to let the beautiful mayhem soak in, banged the bottom of my fist on the bar, drained my glass and ordered some more. Who wouldn't want to be a part of this?

The first game of the following season. With a sense of dread we made our way up to our new seats. No swearing in front of other people's children. No standing, no jumping about. No fun.

But for the first time in years I could see all four corner flags and both goals without standing on my tiptoes or shoving people out the way. Not only that but I was surrounded by enthusiastic, noisy drunks who leapt about hugging strangers and who swore and screamed like the mad bastards they are. I was, and still am, thrilled to be there. I wouldn't go back to standing if you begged me.

CHAPTER 38

Dancing With Wolves

Slowly, without you really noticing when it happens, a football season stops being fun and starts becoming a test of mental endurance. There's not a switch that flicks you from one to the other, it's a gradual increase of pressure that means all you think about, all you care about and all you can concentrate on is the increasing intensity. Even if the season is fizzling out into mid-table nothingness the intensity and frustration increase. If you're actually going for anything; Cup run, promotion, European place, relegation avoidance or once in a while, if you're lucky, a League Championship, it gradually becomes agonising and insufferable.

Everybody lays awake, mentally flicking through League tables, fixtures, goal difference and goals scored. You can try and numb the pain with beer but in the morning it all comes rushing back at you through the hangover fog - there is no getting out.

Sometimes I wonder if, as Newcastle fans, we can't help but care too much. Or possibly we're just not used to competing for honours and we don't know how to cope. I do know that in going for The Premier League Championship in 96 I drank myself to insensibility every night for a month at the end of the season in an attempt to blot out the constant buzz of information in my head - it was a relief when it ended.

It's the time between the matches that's unbearable, at the games the crack with the fans and the rush of seeing the Lads is the easy bit.

10th of April and the sun was beating down on the Black Country. We were standing outside The Goal Post pub, pints in hand, admiring the impressive new stand that had sprung up over the road. Although still not finished, Molineux had been transformed in recent years from a rotting museum piece into one of the most impressive, shiny new grounds in the First Division. Wolves had been there or thereabouts in the race for promotion for a couple of years but, unlike Newcastle, they had decided to invest in bricks and mortar rather than new players. Perhaps they, and not we, were doing things the right way round. Only time would tell.

The Goal Post's regulars turned up to find their bar stuffed to the doors with Geordies. They initially looked pissed off about it but the banter was excellent. Foolishly volunteering to get the next round I found the bar now six people deep. The Landlord, a large, grumpy-faced Villa fan was pouring drinks as fast as he could and looking harassed. "Oi Villa, over ere!" shouted a lad in a gold shirt. "Hang on, there's people before you," growled the landlord.

"No there's not."

"There is now." People laughed and offered more anti-Villa abuse.

"Aston Villa for the League, I say," said I.

"Yes sir, and what would you like?"

(Wahoo) "Six pints of export lager please." The crowd at the bar groaned and complained and another lad in a Newcastle shirt tried it. "Aye, I think Villa are great."

The landlord looked him square in the eye and said, "I think Newcastle are crap." The lad didn't blink or hesitate. "So do I." More laughter and the lad was getting served as I started passing drinks back over the heads of the thirsty to the eager hands of my travelling companions.

We didn't seem to stop laughing. We bought cans at the supermarket and wedged them into the boxes containing the 'Mags' we had brought to sell and Ian bought the most hilariously unappetising looking pie the world had ever seen. By the time we'd sold out of 'The Mag' and stumbled up the steep, shadowed terracing we couldn't have been happier.

Newcastle were inexplicably awful. The worst they had played all season, losing a poor game 1-0 that ended up with Keegan putting "Killer" Kilcline up front as a make-shift striker. A tactic which never, ever worked.

Outside the atmosphere had soured. Ian pulled a micey little bastard in a black and white shirt away from hitting an argumentative and aggressive but aged Wolves fan and supporters snapped angrily at each other. In the car Ian and I bickered angrily, noisily and badly about the unemployed's right not to work all the way back to Newcastle. I rang Alan, the driver whose youngest son was sat in the crossfire, to apologise the next day but he thought it was funny.

It rained all through Easter Sunday, all night, then all the morning of Easter Monday and we were halfway through our first pint in Inventions when the landlord told us the game was off. Portsmouth had won while we were losing at Wolves and then that day cut our lead at the top of the table to a nerve-jangling two points by beating Derby while we listened to the radio, fretted uncontrollably and watched the rain continue to hammer down.

CHAPTER 39

Fear & Loathing In South London

Millwall away at the Old Den and suddenly all my usual travelling companions had really important things to be doing in the North East. Weddings, work, and the need to hide under their beds were suddenly insurmountable barriers that meant, reluctantly, they wouldn't be able to get to Millwall.

Meanwhile, Portsmouth and West Ham were hot enough on our heels for us to be able to smell salty sea-dogs and jellied eels in our sleep. Losing in London could see us knocked off the top of the League the week before we played sunderland. Psychologically this seemed a very bad thing and having to give away my tickets for the game just because I hadn't made any travel arrangements seemed daft.

Fortunately, I bumped into Geoff and Sue at Wolves who were travelling down to London on the Friday night. Somehow this earned me the job of organising the selling of 'The Mag'.

The Friday evening A1 was a bastard nightmare (as per) and I got dropped off an hour late at 9 p.m. before jumping in a cab to an Islington pub to meet an old friend, Shaun, who had reached the stage of rummaging through the last of his change as I tumbled in the door.

Thirsty!

I spent the whole weekend being late and without the mobile phones that have now made such things a breeze I was constantly in danger of being fucked. For example, if I missed Shaun I had nowhere to stay. We got another cab to a cashpoint and then to the Powerhaus in Islington where we ignored the bog-awful Heart Throbs and got drunk in the bar until 2 in the morning.

I woke up on Shaun's floor, pulled my boots on, ate some toothpaste and missed the train to Kings Cross. The London Underground is very similar to the Newcastle Metro system except it's filthy and it's shit and I waited 25 minutes for the next one which meant I was late to meet Joe in the station bar. QPR didn't have a game so he was off to Newbury for the racing. I also met another old friend, Tim, a Tottenham fan and both of them took delight in recounting Millwall horror stories.

Getting dropped off at the gate by the supporters' bus is one thing, wandering in by yourself is quite another. Clearly I was taking my life in my hands. "Whatever you do don't look lost," was their parting advice.

When the crappy transport system finally spat me out in South London I had lost all sense of direction and the same beer that was making my head spin in the sunshine was putting a considerable strain on my bladder. I smiled at the crone guarding the door of the nearest pub. She eyed me suspiciously, then opened the door just enough for me to squeeze into the bar packed with jolly Londoners. I wandered round pretending to look for somebody until I found the bog. The thrill of being behind enemy lines was intoxicating and I even considered a swift pint but I was already well late to meet Geoff and Sue who had the box full of copies of 'The Mag' to sell.

The crone looked me up and down as I approached the door to get out and I felt a rush of panic -the witch could smell the Newcastle on me for sure and the bar full of people, who looked quite normal, were seconds away from turning into cut-throat murdering pirates who would surely skin me alive and toss my lifeless corpse into the street.

She opened the door a half inch, I slithered through and it crunched shut behind me. Now where the fuck is the ground? The Old Den was like Ayresome Park - hidden in a warren of back streets that only local people knew their way through. In a stroke of genius I bought a Millwall fanzine and holding it like Neville Chamberlain coming back from meeting "Herr Hitler" I confidently strode along behind a young couple in blue shirts.

Geoff and Sue were waiting with the 'Mags' and with Dean. I'd met Dean for the first time at Tranmere. By the end of the day he would be my new best mate. Outside we sold fanzines to silent Geordies but once released into their natural environment (an open terrace) they were transformed into a boisterous noise machine and for more than two hours they kept up the most ferocious racket. Dean and I eased through the crowd, negotiated our way round the massive concrete base of a floodlight and found ourselves on the extreme right of the terrace behind the goal. We had 4,000 fans spread along the whole end which was split into fenced-off sections and penned in from the pitch by another fence. The Old Den was a tatty ancient bastard of a ground, seemingly made up of bits of stadiums that other teams didn't want. None of it matched but it was tight and intimidating and the locals were well up for this game.

The home fans singing, "We are Millwall, no one likes us we don't care!" was as daunting and impressive in full voice as anything we saw that season and so was their team. We had our work cut out and while we fans laughed as we sang, "Millwall, Millwall, soft as shite" our team was getting put through the mincing machine. They had an iron grip on the midfield, our forwards were isolated and our defence was getting turned like we hadn't seen in a long time. Within 15 minutes we were losing.

From where we were standing we could see their cross went out of play before it bent back in, hit the top of the post and span into the net. Three sides of the ground exploded.

The black and white horde barely stopped to take a breath and were right back behind the team that was still struggling to find its feet. We managed a couple of tentative attacks but Millwall were irrepressible. A free-kick clattered off Pav's post. The rebound was picked up and whipped back in to Malcolm Allen, who rattled a shot off exactly the same inch of woodwork - the home fans roared and groaned as we hung on for grim death.

In the second half Newcastle were attacking their own fans' end. Killer came on for the injured Howey and, aided by Venison's vicious and immaculate tackling, the defence slammed shut on the Millwall forward line. Bracewell wrestled control of the midfield and with Lee Clark's non-stop running the game was transformed. Raw belief and enthusiasm dragged us back into the game. Cole turned in the area and Clarkie whizzed across him to whip the ball in for 1-1. The eruption behind the goal had us all crashing down the steps, twisting and screaming in the arms of strangers. Cole had chance after chance after chance that he scuffed, sliced or blasted straight at the keeper but he never gave up and eventually twisted in a crowded area and simply passed the ball into the corner of the net.

Me and my new best mate fell down the steps locked together beneath leaping feet, grinning and shouting, oblivious to the pain. Helping each other up, some yards away from where we had been standing, we joined in a bouncing rendition of The Blaydon Races as the Millwall fans sat silent and sulking.

20 minutes left and now we were nervous. Millwall came back at us as their fans urged them on. Our usually composed defence was reduced to lumping the ball clear but we cheered every desperate hoof. Meanwhile Dean couldn't bear

to watch and had his head in his hands. A man in his mid-forties patted him on the back and said, "Howay, bonny lad, we've got this game won."
Dean smiled thinly and looked unconvinced.
Then the whistling started.
Years ago I gave up whistling and, along with the regular lads and lasses around me at St James's, actively discourage it from others. It makes your side panic and encourages the opposition but at this game we whistled until we couldn't breathe.
"Howay ref man, ya'bastard."
A Millwall shot, rippling of net, home fans up...
Side netting. "Jesus!"
We howled out the last of the tension as the ref blew his whistle. People were dancing, clapping, shouting and roaring in each others faces. The players were jubilant and we swapped applause. I came face to face with Mark R and we clasped hands and just shouted - primeval and incomprehensible.

15 minutes later we were still there. The back slapping and high fives had given way to chorus after chorus of "sun'land, sun'land here we come, sun'land, here we come" and then to the thought about getting out. Some people had ran into trouble on the route in. A lad with blood running down the side of his head explained, "a load o'them just fuckin' ran at us. But when we didn't run they stopped an' started hoyin' bottles and bricks. We went after them and they fucked off." Lovely. And the police had surely given them time to organise another ambush afterwards in delaying our departure.
We left the ground and trudged through the streets littered with broken glass and shattered car windows in absolute, eerie silence. The place was deserted and the expected Zulu style charge never happened. We sold the last of 'The Mags, I wished my new best mate well and then we saw a couple of young lads from a rival fanzine who were shaking with fear. We always enjoyed a healthy bit of abusive banter so them on the point of soiling themselves cheered me up no end but Geoff, who was parked close (and with all his windows intact), gave them a lift well away from the stadium before abandoning them to the urban jungle. "You'll be alright, man."
Portsmouth had won 1-0 at Notts County so we were two points clear of them and five clear of West Ham. Even if West Ham won all their remaining games we would only need 4 points from 4 games to guarantee promotion.
"Bring on the mackems."

CHAPTER 40

Look Mummy, mackems

Disregarding a loss of life, sunderland winning at St James's Park is just about the most disgusting thing to contemplate in the world. It's bad enough that they're in the ground at all, knowing that the club is going to have to have the whole ground hosed down with industrial strength disinfectant. To have them being happy at our expense is just wrong and you feel violated.

Worse than being at the game, you know they will crawl out from under their rocks in their thousands, with their tongues flicking in the daylight, slimy, disgusting and sporting sly lop-sided smiles for the next hundred years on the strength of that victory.

My first game at St James's Park was the derby match we lost 1-4 in 78. I was possibly the least bothered Mag in the ground, having finally got to a game after endless parent badgering. I was now officially a real hardcore fan and I walked around with my chest puffed out at school on the Monday. And we beat Charlton 5-3 the week after, so where was the harm?

But I was young and naïve and unaware that 25 years later the fuckers would still be harping on about it.

We'd been revved up to play the mackems for weeks - things were as they were supposed to be: us brilliant, exciting and chock-full of goals and confidence, them a rubbish, disorganised mess, fighting against relegation. Both sides had needed a new striker and whereas we had bought Andrew Cole for £1.75 million (young, gifted and fast) they had bought Michael Harford for £200,000 (old, clumsy and virtually immobile).

But the morning of the game my nerves were shot to hell and I was drinking vodka out the bottle, in the bath. Saturday 3 p.m. the weather was perfect for football but the cops had moved the game to midday Sunday and it had been pissing down for about 18 hours. Not only that but Portsmouth beating Wolves on the Saturday had actually knocked us off the top of the League and West Ham had come from

a goal down to see off Bristol Rovers. We had games in hand but.......
It was all too horrible to stay sober.
At the ground we found some solace in the fact that the people responsible for this
fiasco, Her Majesty's Constabulary, were soaked and miserable. At least we were
there by choice. A rumour went round that the game was due to be abandoned,
like the Oxford game had been, but that the police had said the game was getting
played even if the ball boys started drowning. Our confidence was lifted by the
arrival of Bront who had consumed 4 pints of snakebite for breakfast and was, as
ever, bursting with a contagious confidence.
It was still hammering down and the freezing wind pulled at our soaked clothes.
Mad Frankie (who I never saw do anything remotely strange, never mind "mad")
had been selling 'The Mag' for two hours and was drenched through to his blue
skin, shivering violently. We laughed at him and told him he was going to die.

The groundsmen were sweeping gallons of water off the pitch but as the players
ran out to loud, intense and aggressive applause you could see the water splashing
up from under their feet, even on the bits of pitch that looked playable.
We had two major fears: firstly, that we would be winning and the game would be
abandoned and, secondly, that the conditions would help sunderland's brand of
non-football and be to the detriment of our immaculate passing game.
From the start the players of both sides struggled, not knowing if the ball would
stop suddenly in a puddle or skim away.
The insidious Gordon Armstrong threw the ball at Paul Bracewell at a free kick
in the first minute. Armstrong was booked. 5 minutes later he went in violently on
Rob Lee and the ref clearly told him that was his last chance as we screamed for
his dismissal and summary execution. The fouling taken out of his game he had
nothing else to offer. Harford tried to follow in late on Srnicek but to our immense
pleasure Pav cleared the ball cleanly and, with his shoulder, put the lumbering oaf
spinning onto his fat arse.
Kelly, suddenly clean through, only managed a tame shot at Norman, then Terry
Butcher (sunderland player-manager) clumsily manhandled Scott on the edge of
the area and had the bare-faced gall to complain at the free kick given. All well
and good but O'Brien wasn't in the team. "I fancy Sellars from here," said Alan
to my left. I looked at him and scoffed.
Rob Lee ran over it and Sellars bent it over the wall onto the inside of the right
hand post and it went (seemingly) across the face of the goal. We couldn't see for

the sunderland wall. The Leazes End usually goes up on a goal but it was full of mackems so for a second we didn't realise the ball had gone in the net. The players were away in a pack celebrating and the shockwave of delight ripped along the paddocks and benches into the Gallowgate end in a flash.

The noise was ear-rending and the rain forgotten in the pandemonium. Steam was rising off the Newcastle fans.

A fantastic eight man move that Clarkie was involved in twice saw Cole tear past Butcher to cross, Clarkie headed it on and Kelly, at full stretch, just put it over.

Newcastle kept trying to play football but it was difficult and they had a fight on their hands as well, with sunderland clattering violently into challenges. Both sides' fans had reckoned without the tenacity of Scott Sellars. He looked frail and some fans had remained unconvinced but the goal had given him the confidence he needed and he was involved in everything. Tackling, running, always available, never giving the ball away, he was a dynamo and was having his best game of the season.

At half-time we saw the flag for the first time. Keith Barratt and his mates had been collecting money for weeks and we were all eager to see what they had come up with.

While sunderland's fans passed round what was a handkerchief in comparison, in the East Stand a massive black and white striped flag was being unfurled. It was about 80 feet long and 30 feet high stretched out and it rippled majestically along the stand and back again. Then it was skillfully turned over to reveal the immaculate lettering -

NEWCASTLE UNITED, TOON ARMY.

The sheer elegance, beauty and perfection of it had fans cuffing away tears from rain-streaked faces.

The ground staff spent all of half-time desperately sweeping away waves of surface water but the rain was easing off along with our fears of a match abandoned. sunderland, somewhat bizarrely, decided it would be best for them to defend a 1-0 scoreline. Rob Lee headed agonisingly close, Cole just failed to get on the end of a Clark cross and Lee rattled a shot off keeper Norman's enormous nose. Meanwhile on the terraces we sang, "We put Terry Terry Terry Terry Butcher on the dole".

Time crawled on and our fear of a horrible late, fluky, typically scabby sunderland equaliser grew. There were a couple of desperate scrambles that came to nothing but in the last minute they got a free kick.

The ball was looped in as we held our breath.....
.....headed clear but our relief stuck in our throats as the ball came straight back in again.
Offside.

"Yessssssss."

Then, as the Geordie public sometimes do when the team most need it, came the rush of mental steel. All around the ground the crowd were on their feet, singing, pointing and bellowing, "WE ARE TOPPA'THE LEAGUE, I SAID WE ARE TOP OF THE LEAGUE."

The final whistle brought a rapturous rush of emotion and relief. We roared our throats sore, clapped our hands scarlet and even Paul Bracewell looked pleased.

The soaked fans rammed out the city centre pubs, luxuriating in a vanquished enemy, grinning like wanking gibbons and safe in the knowledge that we had three games left to get the one point that would see us promoted and that the Championship was virtually in the bag.

We stumbled home to hot curries, cold beer and dry clothes and watched the whole match again. Jim Smith, manager of Portsmouth, was co-commentating and despite the fact that it would be in his team's best interest for Newcastle to lose, he clearly and unashamedly wanted us to win, from demanding Armstong's dismissal in the first minute to virtually purring with satisfaction at the end - bless him.

We needed the points so badly that at the time 1-0 was enough. But we all know in retrospect that the weather got sunderland out of the serious twatting they so richly deserved.

The fact that they spent most of the game defending a 1-0 loss and many of the following years hiding in a different division so we couldn't thrash them sideways is something the media ignores. We know it. They know it.

It would be another 10 years before we witnessed another home victory over sunderland who did the footballing equivalent of quivering under the table for 5 of those years.

On Saturday September the 21st 2002 Newcastle, a mere 3 days on from a trip to Kiev in the Champions League, walked the derby 2-0. With another Champions League game the following Tuesday, Newcastle, basically, did all they had to do and passed the ball around for the last twenty minutes. Again we celebrated hard but again they didn't get the mauling we need and they deserve to see. Perhaps that's just greed on my behalf because, damn, it feels fine - it just nags a bit.

CHAPTER 41

Shirts Of Blue

Contrary to media opinion, football fans love kit changes. They love merchandise in general: from hats to training tops, to gloves, shorts, polo shirts, kit bags right down to their NUFC underpants and shin-pads. But a new shirt coming out gives us all a tingle of excitement.

The merchandise at Newcastle, like everywhere else, was tatty and awful for years. The club shop seemed almost embarrassed to have anything other than replica shirts. There would be nothing else except cheap pens, mugs and a T-shirt with a cartoon on it that looked like a tramp punching Al Jolson that was actually supposed to depict Willie MacFaul shaking hands with Mirandinha.

When the new shirts came out there was always a clamour from fans but the media's first attitude to any change is to find somebody, anybody, who objects. "It's only been three years since the last new shirt - it's a rip off."

This left the administration in such a state of paranoia about being seen to be actually trying to make money that when the club sponsorship changed from "Greenalls" back to the S&N blue star, chairman Gordon McKeag turned up on the local news announcing that the club would be giving away a black strip with a blue star on it that fans could sew on over the old sponsor's name. With the new logo stitched into place the shirts looked awful and the wearer looked fuckin' stupid, and yes, I did have one.

Still sensitive to claims of profiteering under John Hall's regime in 1994, the club found itself needing a third choice kit to wear at Sheffield Wednesday. They at once said the kit would not be replicated and sold to the fans. Proof that fans love new shirts was provided by an instant and massive demand for the kit, despite it being a gaudy green colour.

The club now understands that fans like spending money they can't afford on club stuff so the club shops are magnificent and the stuff they sell is stylish and well-made.

It's designer casualwear by the back door and it's snapped up by the armful, even by people who scoff at designer labels.

"But it's over-priced," claim consumer watchdogs. Oh please, have you seen the price of a Calvin Klein shirt or a DKNY dress - and which garment do you think is going to see the most action?

"But kids demand all the new stuff and parents can't cope with the financial burden."

Bugger off and tell somebody who gives a fuck, will you? I've got no sympathy with that argument whatsobastardever. Firstly: kids are expensive, full bloody stop; you knew that before you had them. Secondly: who was it who wedged them into a NUFC romper suit two seconds after they were free of the womb? Who deliberately infected them with the football virus by allowing them to be born in Newcastle? They didn't ask to be born at all and they didn't ask to be born here; it's your fault so get your fuckin' purse out. Also if you've raised spoiled little whiny bastards who won't be told "no" don't come crying to me and certainly don't sit near me on the bus or on the plane or in a restaurant either. Thirdly, and most importantly, would you rather they asked for a sunderland or a Man Utd shirt instead?

The timing of the release of the new home and away kits was immaculate. A blank weekend after we had stuffed the mackems, with promotion and the Championship all but nailed on. On top of this, compared to the old barcode-style home shirts and yellow and green away kit, the new stuff looked excellent. Bolder black and white stripes on the home kit and a magnificent electric blue away kit. Also for the first time fans could get a name and a number printed on the back. The queue at Gallowgate was monstrous and by lunchtime the town was swarming with people of all ages decked out in new gear.

There was a nine day gap after the sunderland game. We had been due at Grimsby the following Saturday but the police didn't want Newcastle fans staying in Cleethorpes over what was a Bank Holiday weekend so that game was moved to the following Tuesday. The police had also brought in a ridiculous 10 day rule for replays which meant the rained-off Oxford game couldn't be shuffled back a couple of days but had to be wedged in before the last game of the season. That game would be on the Thursday, two days after the game at Grimsby. Fortunately for Newcastle, and much to the disgust of Portsmouth and West Ham, our last game of the season was moved back 24 hours so it could be shown live on T.V. But this would mean we would come out of the ground to closed pubs. All day drinking was introduced six days a week in 1988 but pubs still had to shut on a Sunday afternoon.

New shirts in bags, Wifey & I went to get the Metro home from the Central Station. There we, and a lot of passing Mags, took the time to shake hands with Portsmouth fans on their way to sunderland. It would be to Newcastle's benefit if Pompey lost but sheer malice and spite had us patting them on the back and wishing them well.

At the last hurdle, the wheels came spinning off Jim Smith's promotion bandwagon. Portsmouth crashed 4-1 and had two players sent off. The next day West Ham seized their chance and won 3-1 at Swindon.

On the following Tuesday I lovingly removed my beautiful new blue shirt from the wardrobe for the first time, thinking most fans would choose the new black and white shirt.

Grimsby was a mass of blue. A few people clung to the old yellow and a sizeable proportion had black and white on but the abiding memory of the fans hanging banners on the railway bridge, kicking footballs around the beach and pouring heroic amounts of beer down their necks is a night swamped by a dark electric blue.

Officially there were 14,000 at Grimsby with Newcastle having an allocation of 3,600. Both figures were a nonsense and Newcastle fans were in packs all around the ground.

Warmed up by the trip down, which had involved baiting and gloating at the mackems on their way to defeat at Tranmere, we were in full-on party mood, singing that daft "Championi, Championi, Away Away Away" song (which I'm told translates into a song about mushrooms in Spanish) and wondering how in hell we were going to see any football through that daft fence.

It was an exhausting and annoying experience battling constantly for a view of the ball, having to contend with stanchions, fans climbing the fence and the fact that we were packed in solid, but at least we were there.

Grimsby did themselves credit and it was a hard fought 0-0 at half-time. Rob Lee had battered a shot off a post and the Grimsby keeper had made an exceptional save from Clark but the sides were evenly matched.

Grimsby kicked off the second half and immediately lost the ball. Rob Lee was racing towards us "GO'WAN!!!" we roared and fought and scrambled with each other for a view. Lee slid in Cole, I leaned into the bloke next to me and his arm went across my face. I yanked it clear as the tight mob behind the goal pressed eagerly forward. Cole expertly cut across the last defender, drew the keeper and slid the ball into the corner of the net just feet from where I was fighting for a view. It was the last thing I saw of the pitch for several minutes. The pressure caused a gate in the fence to burst open and fans spurted out onto the pitch. Other people were scrambling up the fence while the rest of us jumped and clawed all over each other in a clamorous mob of blue, black and white.

It took a few minutes to clear the pitch of the wounded and over-excited, time the away fans used to build up a deafening wall of teeth-loosening noise that had the hair on your arms and neck prickling.

Grimsby proudly fought back but Newcastle (Bracewell and Venison in particular) didn't look prepared to concede an inch. Beresford was up and down the line constantly and Lee Clark who had played in every single game of the season was running non-stop. The lad was everywhere and this allied to the fact that Kelly and Cole were a constant menace to the Grimsby back line meant we were always threatening to break. Cole went clean through - the keeper made a great save. With surely only seconds remaining Clark burst through on the edge of the box and was brought down. "Penalty, free-kick, line-out, scrum, drop ball, anything, just keep the bastard thing up here. Why are these fuckers trying so hard, dammit?" The ref waved play on and Grimsby were bursting back at us.

Fans were praying and whistling for the end, then, in what turned out to be the 7th minute of stoppage time Kelly broke clear on the left (our right). He raced wide and out of my line of vision. I scrambled desperately but it was hopeless so I just bit my lip and held my breath. "YEEEEEEAAAAAAAAAASSSSS!!!!!!" came the roar and the jolt that went through the crowd was all I needed to know. Through a gap I saw the players swamping Kelly before being crushed under the flailing, ecstatic mob.

On the final whistle fans immediately infested the pitch and the players were rushed off. We sang, we clapped, "Who The Fuck Are Man Utd" was heard for the first time. We embraced and clapped and sang some more until the pitch was cleared and the team came back out to celebrate with us. Now I was clamped manfully to the fence, the view of players dancing, waving and picking up people's thrown scarves was perfect.

Back at the car everybody was hoarse from the singing. Mark had been promised an executive ticket and had turned up in smart trousers, a shirt and tie but the ticket turned out to be for standing in the Grimsby end which we all thought was hilarious.

When I turned up that afternoon with a bag full of cans my fellow car dwellers looked at me like I was some sort of degenerate alcoholic. Now they greedily grabbed and guzzled them and we gibbered and laughed on the long journey home.

Shattered and pissed I stumbled up the stairs and took off my new shirt to find the bastard fence had snagged it. I was appalled. Wifey, in an attempt to make me shut the hell up, pointed out that few other people would have such a shirt and then, thrilled with my new battle scar, I crawled into bed.

A second later I was flat out.

CHAPTER 42

Black and White

sunderland fans often accuse Newcastle fans of being arrogant, that we believe we are naturally better than them, that even if they finish higher in the League or if they are in a higher League altogether, we refuse to accept that they are the better team.

It's absolutely true - guilty as charged.

Apart from the fact that we know that sunderland is a dump and many of its inhabitants are unwashed, inbred halfwits who smell like damp goats, look at us man!

Black and white looks cooler than red and white. It's a fact. We turn up for a game and even before a ball is kicked we have the swagger of knowing that we look better than them or anybody else.

50,000 Newcastle fans gathered in the same place is the most spectacular sight in football. We make sunderland fans look like a warehouse full of tatty old deckchairs.

Black and White is as cool as you can get - it's Bogart in "Casablanca", Monroe in "Some Like It Hot", Marlon Brando in "The Wild Ones" and a triumphant Ali standing over the floored Sonny Liston.

The coolest start to any film in the last ten years is when the cast of Reservoir Dogs walk out the restaurant together to rob the bank. They look so fuckin' great because they are wearing black and white. If they were wearing red and white they would look like clowns going to the fuckin' circus.

In nature black and white rules. Lets face it, a badger would be nothing but a big bloody rat if it didn't have such a fantastic looking head. The sharpest dressed animal on the Serengeti? The zebra. And what's the coolest looking animal on God's good earth? Siberian tiger - black and white stripes. I rest my case.

The Toon saw off Oxford 2-1 on the Thursday, Clarkie scored from distance and Cole missed a couple of sitters then scored an "Ooyafucka". Sometimes when a goal is scored so fast and dispatched so brutally it's the only sound a fan can make. He swivelled in the area and cracked the ball viciously into the roof of the net and our ghast was still flabbered when Oxford got a goal back.

We sat twiddling our thumbs on the last Saturday of the season. West Ham inched past Portsmouth thanks to having scored one more goal over the entire season.. sunderland got stuffed 3-1 at Notts County but survived relegation by a solitary point.

On the Sunday the town was rocking like a bastard. All the bars were crammed full of excitable black and white crazy people. Getting into some of the pubs was impossible and getting to the bar was a nightmare. But the sun was scorching and if one bar was full, so what, there were others.
At the ground Lindisfarne played on the half-built new Leazes End while professional Geordie, Newcastle's answer to Cilla Black, Mr Alan bloody Robson, exhorted the crowd to "make some noise". The irritating bastard, we come here every other week, we know what to do.
2,000 fewer Newcastle fans got into the game because our club inexplicably gave Leicester the   biggest League allocation apart from sunderland all season. Bear in mind that a year beforehand Leicester had caged 1,800 of us in, pelted us with coins and pies and had then tried to blame us for the near riot that their fans started - it seemed a bit over-hospitable.

The team came out early in their magnificent new all-black training gear to accept the two trophies; the old First Division trophy that Liverpool used to wave about a lot and the new First Division trophy. The massive flag rippled along the East Stand and Alan Robson squealed "make some noise" for the 500th time and tried to start another Mexican wave. We didn't need it, the energy of everybody's celebratory attitude was powering through the sun-drenched, if windy, afternoon.
The new shirts looked great on the fans - on the team they looked superb. Longer shorts, shirts with bolder stripes and the players names on the back. And black and white numbers replacing the massive red ones we'd been used

to. Sharper, cleaner solid: pure Newcastle United. Fantastic.

Perhaps it was the pressure being off, perhaps it was the new shirts or maybe it was Keegan moving Barry Venison into the centre of midfield for the first time but for some reason Newcastle were 6-0 up by half-time. The unstoppable whirlwind of passing and movement that had ripped so many teams apart that season blew even harder and faster than anything we had ever seen and no one had any breath left to be taken. Newcastle simply swarmed all over Leicester. Kelly shot, keeper saved, Cole gobbled up the rebound. 1-0. Lee to Cole, Cole backheel to Lee, difficult angle, 2-0. Cole ran down and robbed a defender, tapped back to Clark, cross to soaring Kelly header, 3-0. Sellars to Clark, cute ball into the path of Kelly who sweeps home, 4-0. Big Pav boot, Kelly gets beyond it and heads back and down for Cole to thump in for 5-0.

Then it really started. We'd heard a couple of choruses of it in the bar and once or twice it misfired at the ground but at 5-0 it caught hold. The "Andy Cole, Andy Cole he gets the ball he scores a goal Andy, Andy Cole" song was rattled out by the whole ground for the first time and it caught on like wildfire. It was exactly what we needed: fast, bouncy and it stuck in your brain like a tumour. Small children, old people and folk barely sober enough to stand couldn't help leaping up and down and clapping as they sang it.

The precision of the passing that led to Robinson crossing for Kelly to head in the sixth was exhilarating.

"Unbelievable" is a word squeaked out by rubbish commentators on a weekly basis. Any goal from more than six inches out and any goal at Old Trafford not scored by Manchester United is apparently "unbelievable". It's not. Being 6-0 up at halftime against a side good enough to make the play-offs? Jumping up and down, clapping and singing and having to stop to shake your head, look at each other wide-eyed before another bout of leaping and clapping. That's unbelievable.

The game finished 7-1.

Cole's hat-trick completed in the second half was enough to ensure that his new song would echo through the city centre until way after the pubs shut. The beautiful East Stand flag was the centre piece of a chaotic conga line that grew and grew as it circled the packed pubs. People were climbing buildings and leaping onto lamp-posts, cheered on by armies of street drinkers. The whole city felt as though it was bouncing. The casualty wards of the hospitals were littered with injured high-jinxers. Smashed ankles of people jumping off stuff, cut feet from running round barefoot in the broken glass - it must have been hellish for the nurses but as the night grew cooler and darker nothing else mattered in the whole world except the glory of the Toon. The people in black and white looked brilliant (even the bloke puking against a wall) and the whole of the Premiership would look at that result and have an uneasy summer. 'Cos Newcastle were coming for them. Ha ha, ya fucker.

CHAPTER 43

N.U.F.C.

Behind the Central Station in the old Post Office building on Orchard Street a group of us were skiving in the basement amongst thirty skips of empty mail bags, drinking coffee and clock-watching, waiting for our meal break so we could bounce into the Telegraph for a pint. Norman, an old timer, dry as sticks, sipped his coffee loudly and said, "Newcastle are doing well?"

"Aye Norman."

"Of course none of them will ever be as good as Wor Jackie Milburn."

"Did you see Jackie play, Norm?"

Like thousands of others I had watched silently as Jackie made his final journey through the streets of Newcastle. Regarded as Newcastle's finest player, excelling in an era when we actually won silverware, the affection and awe Jackie Milburn inspired in people too young to see him play was immeasurable.

Norman's eyes glazed over and he stared into the middle distance. He took a deep breath.

The anticipation hurt.

Norman breathed out.

We were transfixed. My heart nearly stopped beating.

"Naah. I've never been to a football match in me life."

In the middle of the 92/93 season Newcastle United Football Club had its hundredth birthday. Normally this would have been a really big deal. Newcastle United, club and fans, had spent years looking back.

The fact that a landmark of such magnitude could be overlooked was seen as outrageous by some fans and obviously they've got a point. But the fact that the vast majority couldn't give two hoots was a brilliant thing. It's like we'd cut away all the baggage that had been dragging us down: we were a brand new team, building a brand new stadium playing football that none of us had ever seen before.

92/93 was year zero and nothing that happened before that mattered. Our wildest dreams were being outstripped by reality and we were too busy hanging onto the ride of our lives to consider where we had come from.

Kevin Keegan and John Hall forged the beginning of a vision that, even though they are both gone, we are still reaping the benefits of today. That season put a belief in our hearts and a swagger in our step that set a benchmark for what we could expect and demand. It is possible to be wildly exciting and reckless and be successful - we can expect entertainment and points.

Lets not forget that the first year of The Premiership was mostly the same dull old dish-rag that had been blowing about in the wind for years. Entertaining or successful, that was the choice teams had been making and most appeared to believe that being tedious to watch was OK as long as they didn't get relegated. Man Utd won that first Championship ahead of Aston Villa, and to be fair they were good but every other team in that League was rubbish or boring. And generally both. Compare the players playing for Arsenal, Leeds, Liverpool, Chelsea or anybody else in 93 and then look at those teams now. Newcastle turned up with an attitude and a blueprint that other teams tried to grab for their own. Some teams thought it was all about spending money. They were wrong, it was about re-inventing yourself with a positive attitude. But you also needed the bollocks and a city full of rabid fuckin' maniacs to really make it work.

Obviously Sky Television thought Newcastle United exploding onto the scene was the best thing that ever happened to them - simply because we were.

After a few early hiccups in August 93 we swashbuckled through that division and qualified for the UEFA Cup in our first year. Cynics scoffed and said we would have to adapt our game to play in Europe and we went out and won 5-0 away to Royal Antwerp.

Our enemies point at an empty trophy cabinet. But I point to second place in the League twice. Two Cup Final appearances and six qualifications for Europe in ten years. We've been to Wembley 4 times, we've seen Newcastle play competitive matches in Barcelona, Rome and Turin. Yes, I'd walk to Wales to see us win the damned League Cup, but are we failures?

Like shit we are. Getting battered 4-0 at Southend, spending our time hating teams like Cambridge - that's Loserville and we don't live there anymore. Not winning the Championship in 1996 cut us all to the bone and Keegan never recovered mentally while Newcastle manager but I still refuse to believe we've failed.

Who of us got into supporting Newcastle United to see us waving some gaudy pot about anyway? Only the sheep and social inadequates who flock from miles away to Old Trafford and Anfield think football is just about seeing your team win silverware.

It's more to do with the crack, the laugh, the beer and what happens on that day and that match alone. Next week can bring what it will - if Newcastle play well and win today I'll be happy. If they don't we'll have a beer, take the piss out of each other and be back for the next game.

Do you remember choosing to follow this team? I don't. You just do and while some weak-minded souls can, and do, change the team they follow - we don't. That's partly because we are too pig-headed and proud of our increasingly beautiful city, its cultural heritage and our own regional identity, but it's mostly because going to the match with Newcastle fans is brilliant. Being in a strange city surrounded by friends or being in a familiar place and embracing a total stranger - it's the best feeling in the world. For all that has changed in football, and in Newcastle itself, that rush you get when the ball rips into the net for a Newcastle goal remains one of the finest things in the world and we want to be there when it happens.

Cheers
BF